David Lee is a professor of psychology at Hagerstown Junior College in Maryland. He has taught fly fishing to beginners of all ages for many years, and he conducts a guide service during the fishing season. He has made a series of television programs on fly fishing for the West Virginia Department of Natural Resources, and his articles on fishing appear frequently in leading magazines.

A Basic Guide to Fishing

For Freshwater Anglers of All Ages

David Lee

Illustrations by Daniel D. Feaser
Photographs by David Guiney

PRENTICE HALL PRESS
New York   London   Toronto   Sydney   Tokyo

Published in 1987 by Prentice Hall Press
A Division of Simon & Schuster, Inc.
Gulf + Western Building
One Gulf + Western Plaza
New York, NY 10023

Originally published by Prentice-Hall, Inc.

PRENTICE HALL PRESS is a trademark of Simon & Schuster, Inc.

Library of Congress Cataloging-in-Publication Data
Lee, David, 1942-
    A basic guide to fishing.

    Bibliography: p.
    Includes index.
    1. Fishing I. Title
SH441.L4 1983   799.1′2   83-10946

ISBN 0-13-062307-5 (pbk.)

Manufactured in the United States of America

10 9 8 7 6 5

First Prentice Hall Press Edition

In memory of my father

Robert C. Lee

(1920–1972)

Contents

Foreword

Studies show again and again that somewhere in the neighborhood of 80 percent of the fish are caught by about 20 percent of the fishermen. Said in another way, only 20 percent of the fish are caught by 80 percent of all fishermen.

What makes a good fisherman? It's not a simple answer—obviously. An experienced trout angler may be completely unskilled if he seeks another species. Tackle varies for many kinds of fish and even for the same species, but under varying conditions—and even at different times of the year. Surface lures will take few bass when the water is chilly, and yet those same lures are deadly in the shallows of a summer morning or evening.

Even the proper hook you use is critical. A fish with a small mouth can't be expected to take in a large hook; a hook with the wire too light will straighten and allow a trophy to escape. Equipment that functions well when it's new may fail when fighting a heavy fish, unless you know how to maintain that tackle.

All of this may discourage someone from taking up the sport. But it is the solving of problems that makes fishing so fascinating to most of us. True, we need to succeed enough to keep us encouraged, but when we find a problem that needs solving—that's when we get the extra spice from fishing. Good anglers continue to learn. Learning is enjoying, and the more you learn about fishing, the more fun it becomes. No one catches fish every time.

David Lee has come as close as anyone to answering many of the questions basic to angling. His orderly presentation of *A Basic Guide to Fishing For Freshwater Anglers of All Ages,* causes the novice to think about the subject in an orderly fashion, gaining leapyears of experience on the person who started fishing on his own.

With this book you will be able to judge what kind of tackle will suit your needs. It also will aid you in evaluating the good and bad points in tackle: rods, reels, lines, lures, etc. Fishing line is just fishing line to most people. But Dave explains that this isn't true. With a better appreciation of the various lines you will be able to select the ones best for you.

No hook out of a box is sharp enough to fish with. A fish must grab a minnow with tough spines on its back and eat it; or it must crush a crayfish shell before it swallows the bait. Its mouth must be rubber-tire tough. You need to know how to sharpen hooks and Dave tells you how.

Much has been written about how to "read" the water to determine where you should be fishing. Dave explains why fish hold in specific locations and makes it simpler for you to decide where to make your presentation. You can fish off the bank, wade the lake or stream, fish from a boat, canoe, or other craft, and the book tells you why and how to use the various methods.

Two types of lures are used for fishing: artificial and live bait. There's a heap of information on both—enough to let you get started in the right manner.

The glossary will be one of the most important parts of the book. Beginners don't know the terms, and if you're going to get involved, you need to understand the language of fishing.

No book will make a fisherman out of you, but this one goes as far as any in helping get started and to learn more about the sport. If you're new to fishing, or want to get involved in the sport, this book will be your bible for the next few seasons.

LEFTY KREH

Preface

There's an image that most of us carry in our mind's eye: a barefoot boy with a cane pole and a can of worms, a bobber floating placidly on the surface of a quiet stream, a faithful dog asleep under a shade tree. Perhaps we first saw the picture on an old calendar or in a sporting magazine, or perhaps that boy was once ourself, in which case we know the image best of all. Whatever the source, that mental picture is one that angler and nonangler alike associate with fishing.

Fishing is much more than the clichés suggest. Certainly it is not always the sleepy pastime conveyed by the cane pole and bobber image. The wonderful thing about fishing is that it can be any way you like it—simple or complicated, vigorous or relaxing, inexpensive or extravagant. But whatever form it takes, fishing is always satisfying to those who love it.

And a lot of people love it. It's possible that one of the reasons you're getting interested in the sport is because you have friends who are confirmed anglers. In fact, if your circle of family and friends is statistically typical, one out of every four people you know is a fisherman—and that comes to fifty-four million Americans, far more than participate in any other sport or hobby.

Fishing is a sport that both sexes can enjoy. Thirty percent of the nation's anglers are women, and more are joining the ranks every day. A women's professional bass fishing circuit provides tournament competition to women who enjoy it.

Fishing is not guilty of age discrimination either. Twelve million anglers in the United States are younger than sixteen, and six million, nearly half of them women, are in the fifty-five and older age bracket. Handicapped Americans are getting involved, too. One of the most welcome developments of the past few years is the creation of fishing facilities for anglers in wheelchairs; there are now hundreds of such facilities nationwide.

In short, there's something in fishing for nearly everyone to enjoy. It is the goal of this book to make you familiar with the kinds of fishing that are available to you and to give you some of the basic skills you'll need to get started on your own. But a book is only a beginning resource. You'll get help from many experienced anglers if you'll only ask—most fishermen like nothing more than giving a hand to a beginner. And the fish will teach you a lot, too, although perhaps more reluctantly than your fellow anglers.

Wherever you live, there is some kind of fishing available, usually many different kinds. I hope you find your kind and come to enjoy it as much as those of us who are already addicted.

Acknowledgments

This book would not have been possible without the help of a great many people, some of them close to me and some whom I have never met personally. All have played their part in making this project a reality.

I received wonderful cooperation from some of the leading manufacturers of fishing tackle and outdoor products and the people who represent them. I am indebted to Dick Jennings and Leon Chandler and the Cortland Line Company; Dave and Judy McCann of Fly–Ryte; Debra Wilner and Early Winters, Ltd.; Peggy Koelble and Flambeau Products Corporation; Nancy Grimes of Chinook Sports, Ltd.; The Stearns Manufacturing Company; Stephen Peterson and Linda Martin of Wright & McGill (Eagle Claw hooks and tackle); Chuck Holly and Shakespeare; Brad Biddle and Mitch Falk and Abu–Garcia; Dick Kotis of Fred Arbogast Company; Jerry Gomber of Shimano American Corporation; T. Layton Shepherd and Sheldon's, Inc. (Mepps lures); Dick Gaumer and Fenwick/Woodstream; Rex Gerlach and Daiwa; Chuck Roberts and Zebco; Johnson Reels, Inc.; The Russell Moccasin Company; Neva Hull and James Heddon's Sons; Gabrielle Hatch and

Harrison–Hoge Industries (Panther Martin spinners and other lures); Guillaume Sacre and The Danner Shoe Company; Dan Gapen of Gapen's World of Fishin'; Dennis Phillips and The Coleman Company; Patty Buck and The Nordic Boat Company; Thane Smith of Lowrance Electronics; Pete Anastasi and Nan Rollison of the U.S. Fish and Wildlife Service, Department of the Interior; and Gil Radonski of the Sport Fishing Institute.

A number of prominent anglers from across the country took the time to share with me (and with the reader) some of their favorite places to fish. My thanks to Jim Corbin, Dan Gapen, Rex Gerlach, Eric Price, Tom Rosenbauer, Dick Kotis, and Ray Scott.

David Guiney's photographs clarify and illuminate the text. All authors should have such a talented brother-in-law. Dan Feaser's illustrations give the book life. After seeing Dan's work in my earlier book, *Fly Fishing*, my editors at Prentice-Hall made it clear that Dan should illustrate this book, too. I didn't need prodding.

My work on the manuscript was aided by a number of readers who took the time to look over early drafts and offer suggestions and comments. Walt Malinowski and Doug Barrick of Lord Fairfax Community College are both experienced anglers and teachers, and their suggestions improved the book. My friend and fishing companion Ben Schley took time from his hunting and fishing to read the manuscript and to encourage me. Ben's writing is like his fishing: relaxed, graceful, and competent. I should like to be more like him in both, and I look forward to the appearance of his own book in the future.

My brother Paul read and reread the manuscript with extraordinary care, and his suggestions have improved this book as they did *Fly Fishing*. Paul cares not a whit for fishing, but a great deal for me. I appreciate his contribution and the affection that motivated it.

Finally, my wife Katherine and our daughter Meg supported me in every possible way during the long process of putting this work together. Meg's many little kindnesses and continuous offers of help (most of which were accepted) converted some of the sheer drudgery into pleasure. And Katherine's skill in editing is exceeded only by her ability to moderate my wilder flights of fancy.

1

The Essentials: Hooks and Lines

So you've decided to take up fishing. If you're a typical beginner, your first inclination will be to buy a rod and reel. That's almost universal practice, and it often results in some horrible mismatches between equipment and the actual requirements of a given fishing situation.

You should choose your tackle based on the types of baits and lures you intend to fish, the places where you plan to fish them, and the species of fish you will seek. Only after considering these questions can you choose the right outfit. Rods and reels are not all alike. As you'll see in subsequent chapters, four basic types of tackle are available: bait (or plug) casting, spinning, spin casting, and fly. Each type functions in a special way and is best suited to a particular type of fishing and to certain baits and lures.

The best place to begin making your tackle decisions is where our primitive ancestors began—with the hook and the line. The hook specifies and defines the type of lure or bait used, including size, weight, and design. The line in turn is chosen to match the bait or lure being offered to the fish. Then, and only then, should you decide on the reel to store the line and the rod with which to cast it.

The Hook

The fishhook is one of mankind's oldest tools. Anthropologists believe that the first tool that caught fish with a line was not a curved hook as we know it today, but a straight piece of stone or bone, sharpened on each end, which was imbedded in a bait and then pulled crosswise in the fish's throat after being swallowed. The disadvantage of such a hook was that it had to be completely swallowed to be effective. You won't fish long before you'll learn that hooks are more often ejected than swallowed by fish. The development of a bent hook that could penetrate mouth tissue soon after being ingested was a big improvement over the straight version.

The bent hook made from bone probably appeared at the dawn of the Neolithic period somewhere in the Near East. The first metal hooks were of copper, about 5,000 B.C. A thousand years later, tin was added to copper to make bronze, and the Bronze Age began. Bronze was a much sturdier metal than copper, and fish hooks were among the first implements made from the new metal. Iron technology followed, and iron fishhooks were in use centuries before the birth of Christ.

Today the centers of fishhook manufacturer are in Norway, France, Great Britain, and the United States. The modern fishhook derived from the needle industry in England in the seventeenth century. A hook is basically a bent needle with a ring at one end and a barb at the other.

Literally thousands of different sizes and styles of fishhooks are available today, and it would be impractical to discuss even a small number of them here. We can, however, take a look at the parts of a typical fishhook and describe the variations that may be found in them, the reasons for the variations, and the advantages and disadvantages of each type.

Figure 1–1 shows a modern fishhook and its parts.

THE POINT

Hook points may be long or short, straight or curved, hollow-ground or triangulated, aimed up toward the shank or down away from it. Whatever their shape, though, they must all be sharp. More fish are probably lost to dull hooks than to any other factor, and most mass-produced hooks don't come out of the box as sharp as you can make them with a little effort. You can buy hook hones in tackle shops for sharpening the

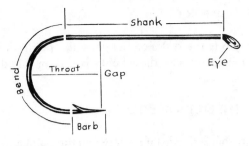

FIGURE 1–1
A typical fishhook

small hooks and fine-grit files in hardware stores for touching up the big ones.

Some hooks are angled at the bend so that the point is not in line with the shank. This increases the effective hook gap, but it also means that the point no longer follows the pull of the line in a direct line. Some anglers think that offset points hook better; some don't. Looking down the shank from the hook eye, a point offset to the right is said to be *kirbed,* while one offset to the left is called *reversed.* Offset points are not found on hooks used on lures. They are designed for bait fishing.

THE BARB

The barb is the portion of the hook that keeps the point from backing out once it penetrates the fish. The barb is made by nicking the steel and raising a portion of it. Since this necessarily weakens the hook at that point, the barb cut should not be too deep.

Barbs may be low or high. Low barbs penetrate easily; therefore, they are a good choice for delicate fishing with light tackle where the angler can't really slam the hook home when the fish strikes. High barbs, on the other hand, hold better once buried, making them suitable for fishing with heavier gear.

More and more anglers are fishing with barbless hooks, at least some of the time. If you plan to release your fish (and catch-and-release fishing is growing in popularity), barbless hooks are the way to go. You can buy barbless hooks or you can modify standard barbed hooks by using needlenose pliers to bend down the barbs. Many fly fishermen fish barbless exclusively. They believe that more fish are landed with barbless hooks, since more are securely hooked to start with because the barbless point penetrates more reliably. The real payoff in barbless fishing comes when you accidentally hook yourself. With no barb, you save a trip to the emergency room!

3

THE GAP (OR GAPE)

The gap is the distance between the point and the hook shank. Most manufacturers size their hooks based on this distance.

THE THROAT (OR BITE)

The throat is the distance between the point and the bend. It represents the maximum distance that the point and barb can penetrate.

THE BEND

The bend, of course, refers to the curved portion of the hook. There are many different bend shapes. The most common is probably the round bend, often called the "model perfect" bend. Parabolic bends (not perfectly round) are also common: *sproat* and *limerick* bends are examples of these.

THE SHANK

Length. The shank is the straight portion of the hook between the bend and the eye. Although hooks are usually sized according to the gap, beginners are often confused, because shank length is often a more prominent visual indicator of the overall size of the hook. Shank length, however, varies considerably in hooks of the same nominal size. Shank length in a hook is designated by a system in which the length of a given hook is described in relation to the lengths of shanks of hooks in other sizes. Thus, a hook described as being "2Xlong" has a shank equal in length to a standard hook two sizes larger, and one listed as "3Xshort" has a shank the same length as a standard hook three sizes smaller.

A short-shanked hook may be desirable in bait fishing, because it is easier to hide in the bait and probably will not damage a live bait so much because of its smaller mass. Short-shanked hooks are also used in tying certain flies. Long-shanked hooks are used in tying flies called *streamers* and *bucktails*; these flies represent bait fish and the long shank contributes to the proper silhouette. A long-shanked hook may also be an advantage in angling for fish such as muskellunge and pike, because the long shank holds the line further away from their sharp teeth. Most anglers feel that 6Xlong is the longest practical length, although 8Xlong hooks are occasionally used. One point to keep in mind is that the hook shank acts as a lever once the hook is imbedded, and the longer the lever the more likely that the fish will be able to work the hook loose before being landed.

Shape. A final variation in shank design is shape. Typical is the straight shank, as shown in Figure 1–1. Sometimes you will see *offset shanks,* in which a portion of the shank is bent up or down along with the eye. Offset shank hooks are often used in constructing jigs and in fishing plastic baits. *Hump shank* hooks are designed to be used in lure bodies of wood, cork, or plastic; the hump keeps the shank from turning inside the body material. Finally, *curved shank* hooks are made in many different shapes and are most often used in bait fishing. They may be chosen because they fit the natural shape of a bait or because they are easier to hide in the bait.

Most of the shank variations are also made with additional barbs on the shank to hold the bait more securely on the hook. The Eagle Claw Company makes a whole series of hooks like this, called "Bait Holders."

THE EYE

The eye is the hole through which the line is threaded to attach the hook. The eye is usually formed by bending some of the shank wire around in a circle, but in some large hooks that are made of heavy wire, holes are drilled directly through the metal. Some eyes are oval and some are round. Another variation is the angle of the eye to the hook shank. The common eye style is shown in Figure 1–1 and is termed the *turned-down eye* (t.d.e.). It is found on the majority of single-point hooks. *Turned-up eyes* (t.u.e.) are most often found on very small hooks because the angle of the eye increases the effective hook gap and leads to more reliable penetration. Turned up eyes are also traditional on salmon fly hooks. Finally, some hooks are made with *ring eyes,* in which the eye is not bent, but is in line with the shank. Such hooks are usually attached to lures or used behind spinner blades. All treble hooks, with three points, have ring eyes.

PACKAGING

You may buy your hooks loose, in boxes, or "snelled" on cards. Boxed hooks are packed in boxes of a hundred in the small sizes, in smaller quantities in the large sizes. Snelled hooks are those that come with a length of monofilament already attached, usually with a loop in the other end for attaching to a swivel or a snap. Snelled hooks are used in bait fishing for the most part.

WEIGHT

You should also be aware that fish hooks come in several different weights, based on the thickness of the wire of which they're made. Hooks made from heavy wire sink well; you won't have to use as heavy a sinker if you use this type for bait fishing, and you won't have to weight your fly leader as much if you tie your wet flies on them. Heavy wire hooks also hold well once the barb and point penetrate the fish; they are not as likely to break or straighten out as the light wire hooks. On the other hand, heavy hooks are harder to "set," or penetrate, in the fish's mouth, and they do more damage when inserted in live bait. Light wire hooks are used for dry fly fishing (fishing with flies that float) and for bait fishing with delicate live baits. Light wire hooks are easier to hide in a bait and they penetrate better, especially with light tackle.

The same "X" system described earlier is used to designate wire thickness in hooks. A hook described as "2Xstout" is made of wire usually found in a standard hook two sizes larger, and a dry fly hook described as "3Xfine" is as fine in diameter as a standard hook three sizes smaller.

FINISH

Good quality, freshwater fishhooks are bronzed to resist rusting. Avoid blued hooks—this finish won't last and your hooks will rust quickly. Some hooks are made of stainless steel. These are more often used in saltwater fishing, but they have a few freshwater applications and may be necessary in brackish water fishing where corrosion is a problem. Whatever the finish, hooks and lures should be carefully dried after use before being put away in vest or tackle box.

As you can tell by now, we've come a long way since the curved-bone days. The fishhook would seem to be the simplest element of the angler's gear, but the selection of hooks can have a great impact on fishing success. Yet I'm surprised at how little attention is paid to this most basic of the angler's tools. I've attended dozens of club meetings, banquets, outdoor shows and the like, and I've heard speeches and seen demonstrations on rods, lures, flies, fly tying, reels, creels, waders, boats, and lines, but I've never yet heard or seen a program that gave more than a passing mention to hooks. Nor do I hear anglers talk about hooks when they get together informally to swap stories and ideas. And yet everything depends on the hook.

As you learn to fish, you'll learn which hooks are best suited to the particular fish and conditions in your area. Try to learn which hooks other anglers are using, because *your* fishing begins where all fishing began so long ago—with the hook.

Lines

As is the case with hooks, fishing lines seem simple at first consideration. Nevertheless, you should do some thinking before going out to buy your first fishing line. Among other things, you'll need to make decisions on such variables as breaking strength ("pounds test"), diameter, material type (monofilament or woven line), and color (or, if you prefer, the lack of it). These decisions in turn depend on the type of water you plan to fish and the fish you expect to find there. In this section, we'll talk about the two major types of fishing line from which you'll choose: monofilament or braided fabric. Since the line for fly fishing is a subject in itself, we'll leave it to the chapter on fly fishing.

MONOFILAMENT

As the name indicates, monofilament is a single strand product made of nylon. Monofilament fishing line came into vogue with spinning tackle for which it is especially suited, but, as it has been improved over the years, it has come into favor for casting tackle, too. Your first fishing line will probably be monofilament, and it is likely that you will do most of your fishing with it.

Nylon monofilament is stiffer than other fishing line. "Hard" mono is especially stiff and is used in "shock leaders" (extra strong mono for the last few feet of line before the lure or bait), in snelling hooks for bait fishing, and in the heavy butt sections of tapered leaders for fly fishing. Apart from these specialized applications, stiff monofilament isn't well suited for most fishing. The material you'll buy for your fishing line is "limp" monofilament, which is stiff when compared to fabric line, but limber enough to be cast and respooled on the reel time and time again.

As with hooks, we'll discuss some of the characteristics of monofilament and the variables you'll need to consider when deciding which type, brand, or size to purchase.

Breaking Strength. The breaking strength of monofilament line is always prominently displayed on the package and is expressed in "pounds test," the number of pounds of pull the line will sustain before breaking. For freshwater fishing, you will be choosing line in the range from four to twenty pounds. With a few exceptions, lines are rated by the manufacturers in two-pound intervals.

The actual breaking strength of a line is a little more complicated than the simple numbers would indicate. For one thing, nylon loses some of its strength when wet, so the leading makers usually underrate their lines by a factor of fifteen to forty percent, especially in lines at the lighter end of the spectrum. Since water only diminishes the breaking strength of monofilament by a maximum of ten percent or so, there is a built-in cushion in the rating that you can rely on, especially in the premium brands.

Another factor is the stretch that is characteristic of nylon. Compared to fabric lines, monofilament stretches considerably, especially in the moderate temperatures in which most fishing takes place. This shock-absorbing quality provides an additional safety margin against breaking your line. Finally, modern reels have smooth "drags" that make it possible to play and land a fish much heavier than the breaking strength of the line in use. If you learn to set your drag properly and check it regularly (and I'll explain how in an upcoming chapter), you need have little fear of breaking your line while playing a fish.

Most beginners (indeed, most anglers at all levels of experience) fish with heavier lines than necessary. In the area where I fish most often, the norm is probably ten- to twelve-pound test. But I seldom fish with anything heavier than six-pound line and often use four; and I can't remember when I last broke my line while playing a fish. You don't need heavy line unless:

1. You have a serious, regular chance of hooking really big fish.
2. You fish in waters with a lot of obstructions. Under these conditions you will have to force fish out of heavy weeds or pull snagged baits out of submerged objects, and you'll need a stiff rod and heavy line to do it.
3. You use tackle or techniques that require heavy lines. Plastic worm fishing, for example, usually requires relatively heavy tackle because the hook is buried in the worm, making it weedless. When the fish picks up the worm, the angler's strike must drive the point through the tough worm and into the fish's jaw; this may take three or four hard whacks to accomplish. Most worm fishermen use ten- to eighteen-pound line for this fishing.

Even if you do face conditions like these occasionally, you won't need heavy line all the time.

There are a number of advantages to using relatively light lines in your fishing.

1. With light lines, you can deliver small- and medium-sized lures to fish that are probably used to seeing large ones. The smaller lures, along with the fact that the light line itself is less obtrusive, could increase your success.
2. With lighter lines, you can use lighter tackle, which is not only more sporting, but more pleasant to use over the course of a long fishing day.

3. If you use light lines for bait fishing, you can also use lighter sinkers and smaller bobbers, hooks, and other hardware.

In short, the trick to challenging and fun fishing is finding what test line you really need, then getting that and nothing heavier. You can find out what's best in your area by consulting an expert angler. If you can't do that, you can come close to the ideal by asking the local sporting goods dealer what weight line he sells most often. Then select one that is forty percent lighter.

Diameter. Diameter, of course, designates the thickness of the line. Generally speaking, you want the smallest diameter you can get in your chosen pounds test. Small diameter line casts better than thicker line because of reduced reel friction and air resistance. With small diameter line, you can get more line on your reel spool, and your line will be less obtrusive in the water. Since small diameter line sinks better, you will be able to achieve a given depth with smaller sinkers and your sinking lures will run deeper. Keep in mind that premium monofilament usually has the average diameter marked on the box.

Stretch. As mentioned, all monofilament stretches. The amount of stretch that's desirable varies with the conditions. While high stretch helps to absorb the shock that a fighting fish can put on a line, it also makes it more difficult to set the hook. Ultralight spin fishermen like a lot of stretch in their lines, while largemouth bass anglers fishing plastic baits in heavy cover generally do not. While stretch is not specified on the package, the makers of premium monofilament have taken it into account: their light lines stretch more than their heavy ones. Once you're fishing, remember this: A fishing line stretches to its maximum only once, and most of the stretching takes place close to the point where the line is firmly attached. If you've just finished a battle with a heavy fish or finally pulled your lure free from an underwater snag, it's a good idea to cut off the last few feet of line and reattach your bait or lure.

Abrasion Resistance. Abrasion can reduce the breaking strength of a line by half, and monofilament is subject to abrasion from many quarters. Since most abrasion takes place close to the lure or bait, it's prudent to cut off the last few feet of your monofilament line a couple of times during the fishing day. You might want to do it more often than that if you're fishing under rough conditions or with unusually light line. Because of the abrasion problem, some ultralight fishermen like to use a six-pound shock leader two to three feet long at the end of their two- or four-pound line.

Color. Colored lines are useful under some conditions. Most of the premium lines work by absorbing sunlight and releasing it again. Most popular are the fluorescent lines of yellow, orange, or blue-green. Such highly visible lines may be advantageous in cloudy or muddy water, especially if you're fishing a jig or other lure that is often picked up very softly. Here you have to see your line move to detect a strike. On the other hand, many anglers think that colored lines alarm fish, and there are some studies to support that notion. If you decide to use colored line, it would be a good idea to use a leader of at least six feet of clear monofilament to separate your lure or bait from the visible line.

Memory. Memory is the fisherman's term for the fact that nylon tends to retain the shape it is stored in, and in fishing that shape is coils. The stiffer the "mono" the more it tends to retain the springy shape it assumed when wound onto the factory spool of your reel. Good quality monofilament has less of this tendency to kink than the poor quality line, and it straightens more quickly in use. Memory is not usually a problem with a premium monofilament unless you allow the line to become twisted. You may twist a line if you troll with monofilament (towing a lure behind a slowly moving boat) or if you use a spinning lure without using a swivel to keep the lure from winding up the line. If either of these conditions occurs, you can usually rectify the problem by letting the last fifty feet or so of line (with no lure attached) trail downstream in the current or unwind behind a moving boat. If you're in a currentless area and without a boat, you can get the line unwound by wading slowly trailing the line behind you.

Inexperienced fishermen often twist a monofilament line badly by winding the reel handle against resistance. Never do this. Don't wind against a snag and don't fight a fish by winding it in. You fight a fish with the rod by "pumping," that is, by lifting the rod and drawing the fish toward you. The reel is wound only to recover slack created by the pumping maneuver, usually as the rod is lowered to begin another pumping motion.

Premium Quality. I recommend that you buy and use premium quality monofilament fishing line. Most such lines are prominently marked as premium, and Figure 1–2 shows some of the major brands of monofilament, along with some braided lines. Premium line costs a little more, but for your investment you get small diameter, high strength, controlled stretch, abrasion resistance, and peace of mind.

Filling Your Reel With Line. Monofilament should be wound on the reel under slight tension so that it will spool properly and lay evenly. Your dealer probably has a spool-filling device that will do a perfect job of filling your reel; if so, let him do it. If not, get a friend to hold the line spool by inserting a pencil through the hole. Thread the line at least through the first guide before fastening it to the reel. I prefer to put the rod together and bring the line through all the guides, but it isn't absolutely necessary. In either case, make sure that there is adequate tension to make the line wind onto the spool properly. It's a good idea to

FIGURE 1–2 A selection of premium monofilament and braided fishing lines. (Photo by David Guiney)

draw the line between two fingers as you wind or have your friend add a little resistance by holding a finger against the turning edge of the spool.

Filling the reel properly is essential to smooth, long, and accurate casts. Spinning reels should be filled to about one-eighth inch of the edge of the reel spool. Casting reels usually have a mark on the spool to designate the proper line level, but if the one you have does not, fill the spool to the point where it begins to flare outward. Spin-casting reels are difficult to fill, because you can't see the line going on the spool. Most stores sell prefilled spools to fit these reels, and it's best to fill them that way. These reels usually come from the factory loaded with premium quality line, and replacement spools should be easy to come by.

The capacity of many of today's reels is marked right on the reel housing. These capacities are approximations because of the variation in line diameters, but they can give you a good idea of how much monofilament you need to buy. If there's nothing marked on your reel, you might find the capacity listed on the box or on the printed matter that came inside.

Maintaining and Replacing Your Monofilament Line. Be sure to store your line (and your filled reel) in an area away from strong sunlight. Some of the sun's rays gradually destroy the molecules that impart strength to the line. Temperature extremes should be avoided, as should solvent chemicals, such as petroleum-based products. If you're one of those anglers who likes to carry a rod and reel in your car trunk, count on changing your line often.

Most serious fishermen change lines at least once a season, spooling up afresh as part of their preseason preparation ritual. If you fish a lot, it will be necessary to change more often, because casting will suffer as you repeatedly cut off the abraded few feet at the end of the line each time you fish. Don't try to add new line by knotting it on; that knot might catch in the rod guides the next time out and cost you a fish. The only safe solution is to replace the whole line and fill the spool to maximum again. If you're tempted to grumble as you lay out money for that new line, remember that it's your link to the fish. The money invested in your other gear is wasted if the line fails.

FABRIC LINE

Fabric line is made of several strands of material woven together. Today most fabric line is made of nylon or dacron, with dacron preferred by most anglers, although it is more expensive.

Fabric line cannot be used with spin-casting reels; it will not spool properly inside the closed housing. It is possible to use fabric line on spinning reels, but the improved limpness and reduced memory of monofilament has made this uncommon. Some anglers who fish surface lures with spinning equipment prefer fabric line because the action of the surface lures does not always provide sufficient tension for properly spooling monofilament. On the other hand, most anglers who fish with surface plugs and lures a lot do not find spinning gear ideal for this fishing.

Fabric line is most often used on casting reels. Since it does not spring off the reel like monofilament, it is easier to control and, therefore, easier to use in situations where highly accurate casts are necessary. Since it has little stretch compared to monofilament, fabric line is excellent for fishing in heavy cover and for fish that require jarring strikes by the angler to set the hook. And since fabric line does not twist as badly as monofilament, it is ideal for trolling.

Fabric line is also used as "backing" behind monofilament. If you have a large spool to fill, it will be cheaper to fill most of it with woven line and add monofilament for the actual fishing line. Since fabric line is usually smaller in diameter than monofilament of comparable strength, more of it can be packed on a reel. Most fly anglers use backing behind their fly lines, both to build up the spool and to protect against the long run of a big fish.

In short, the most common use for fabric line today is in specialized fishing situations. Unless you're unusual, you'll start with monofilament and stay with it for most of your angling.

Knots

Whatever line you use, you'll have to tie knots in it, and both the knots you choose and your skill in tying them are important. The perfect fishing knot has not yet been invented, but there are a lot of good ones. We'll introduce a few of them here, and you will undoubtedly learn new ones as your experience grows.

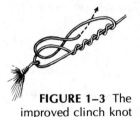

FIGURE 1–3 The improved clinch knot

IMPROVED CLINCH

The improved clinch is probably the most frequently used knot in freshwater fishing. It is used to tie lures to line, line to swivels, flies to leader tippets, and so on. As you can see from Figure 1–3, it's an easy knot to tie. If you moisten it a little as you draw it up, it will hold better.

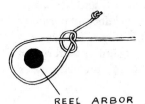

REEL ARBOR

FIGURE 1–4 The arbor knot

ARBOR KNOT

This one gets its name from its purpose: attaching line to a reel. As you can see in Figure 1–4, it is basically two overhand knots, the first tied around the line after it has been passed around the reel spool, the second tied in the end to keep the first from slipping.

SURGEON'S KNOT

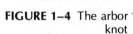

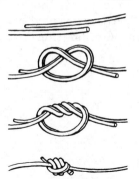

FIGURE 1–5 The surgeon's knot

This knot is used to attach two pieces of monofilament together. It is most often used in making tapered fly leaders, but it is also good when a leader is to be employed in spinning or when a shock leader is needed. The great advantage of the surgeon's knot is that it can be used to join two strands of line that are widely different in diameter. No other simple knot can do this with adequate strength. Again, as you see in Figure 1–5, the overhand knot is the basis for the surgeon's knot. It's so simple that you can tie it in the dark once you have had a little practice.

BLOOD KNOT

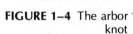

FIGURE 1–6 The blood knot

This is another good knot for joining two pieces of monofilament as long as they are similar in diameter. If the two pieces are more than .003 different in diameter, use the surgeon's knot. As the figure shows, the blood knot is two clinch knots tied back to back. It's a little harder to tie than the surgeon's knot, but it is less wasteful of material, creates an absolutely straight line relationship between the two joined strands, and leaves "waste" strands that stand at right angles to the line, good for making "droppers" on a fly leader to which extra flies or split shot can be attached.

SURGEON'S LOOP

You get a surgeon's loop by tying a surgeon's knot in a single strand of monofilament that has been doubled back on itself. What could be simpler? And, unlike some other loops, this one has a direct line of pull with the line.

FIGURE 1–7 The surgeon's loop

TUBE KNOT

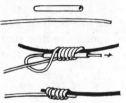

This is the hardest, but it's one you won't have to tie often. It is used mostly for attaching a leader to a fly line. As Figure 1–8 shows, the monofilament is wound around a tube several times, back over itself, then threaded through the tube, the tube is pulled out, and the wraps slowly tightened over the trapped strand. It's a dandy knot and perfectly reliable if properly tied. If you're stuck for a tube, clip the ends off a cotton swab. And coat the knot with Pliobond or a similar waterproof glue when you're finished tying it; it will slide through the rod guides like a dream.

FIGURE 1–8 The tube knot

SUMMARY

These are only six knots out of the hundreds that have been invented and used by fishermen. But these six will satisfy most of the fishing situations

FIGURE 1–9
Here's proof that big fish can be handled on light tackle and light lines. The fish is a carp, and the angler is Minnesota's Dan Gapen. (Photo courtesy Dan Gapen)

you will encounter. Learn them well and practice at home until you can tie them quickly and in a relaxed frame of mind.

Hooks, line, and knots turned out to be a little more complicated than you figured, right? That's why it's a good idea to know something about these essentials and to apply that knowledge to what you know about your fishing situation before you rush out and spend money on rods and reels. Next, we're going to consider the little odds and ends that can make such a difference in your fishing success (in fact, can sometimes make all the difference): sinkers, bobbers, swivels, and the like. We'll also look at some of the ways you can carry your lures and assorted gear ashore, in your boat, or on your back.

CHAPTER **2**

Auxiliary Equipment

If you've ever looked closely at a modern angler's tackle box, you've noted that it contains more equipment than hooks, baits, and lures. It's that additional equipment that we're going to cover in this chapter, along with the tackle boxes themselves and some alternatives. We'll also consider some small accessory items that may not be absolutely essential, but which can make a fishing trip more fun or less hassle.

Sinkers

Sinkers help to hold bait near the bottom of the stream or to suspend it from a bobber. Sinkers are also sometimes used to make lures, flies, and plugs run deeper in the water than they would without added weight. There are many commercially made sinkers, with an especially wide variety available for saltwater fishing, but for freshwater fishing, you **16** need to consider only a few types. Refer to Figure 2–1 for illustration.

PYRAMID

The pyramid sinker is used primarily in bottom fishing where the sinker rests right on the bottom. The bait is attached some distance above, either with a standoff or a three-way swivel. It is best used where the bottom is soft, because the points and angles of the pyramid help the sinker to dig in and hold.

CLINCH-ON TYPE

The clinch-on sinker is usually employed to suspend bait from a bobber. It has a lengthwise slit and two bendable tabs at either end. The line is placed in the slit and the two tabs bent over to secure the sinker. The clinch sinker is usually placed above the bait, often just above the snap swivel that many anglers use to attach a snelled hook to the line. If attached and removed carefully, the clinch sinker can be used several times before the little tabs break off.

DIPSEY AND BANK

The dipsey and the bank are also used for bottom fishing, but they are best for rocky or obstructed bottoms where their rounded shapes help prevent many of the snags that would occur with the pyramid. As you can see in Figure 2–1, the dipsey has a wire loop for attaching the line, whereas the bank has a hole cast in the sinker itself. Most anglers prefer the dipsey, since a tighter and more secure knot can be tied to the wire loop. A snap swivel can also be attached to a dipsey.

FIGURE 2–1 Standard freshwater sinkers. *From top to bottom:* pyramid, clinch-on, bank, split shot, dipsey.

SPLIT SHOT

Split shot is round lead with a split in one side. The line is inserted in the split and the shot is squeezed tight around it. Split shot is used in situations where larger sinkers would be too heavy. For example, they are often used by wading stream fishermen who do not keep their bait stationary, but want to drift it through suspected fish lies. The use of split shot makes it possible to achieve a precise depth, since weight can be added or removed in very small increments. The smallest of split shot are as tiny as bird shot; the larger ones are available with tabs, like the clinch sinker, which make it possible to remove and reuse the shot several times. Fly fishermen especially rely on split shot for much of their underwater fishing.

SLIDING SINKERS

Sliding sinkers are used most often in plastic worm fishing. They are usually bullet shaped with a hole through the middle. The angler threads the sinker on the line and then attaches the hook and buries it in the worm. The sinker slides down right over the knot for casting, but when a fish picks up the worm, the line flows through the sinker with little resistance, allowing the fish to move with the worm without feeling anything unnatural. The sliding sinker worm rig is illustrated in Figure 2–2.

FIGURE 2–2 Sliding sinker slips down over the hook eye on this worm rig. (Photo by David Guiney)

TROLLING SINKERS

Trolling sinkers are designed to hold plugs or lures close to the bottom as they are dragged behind a slow-moving boat. They are usually used along with a three-way swivel; the upper loop attaches to the main line, the lower to the trolling sinker, and the middle loop to the leader which carries the lure. Trolling sinkers have to be carefully designed to avoid spinning and fouling the line and to resist hanging up on bottom obstructions. If you want to troll deep, be sure to use a sinker designed especially for the purpose. (See Figures 2–3a and 2–3b.)

Although there are other types of sinkers, one of the aforementioned designs will suit most freshwater fishing situations.

FIGURE 2–3a Traditional trolling sinkers. *Left:* drail. *Right:* keel.

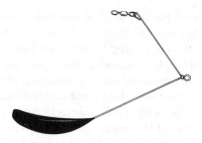

FIGURE 2–3b
Dan Gapen's "Bait Walker" sinker. It can be used for trolling or casting and with live bait and lures of all kinds, even for presenting floating plugs underwater. (Illustration courtesy Dan Gapen)

Bobbers

A bobber has a twofold purpose: It suspends the bait at a selected distance from the bottom, and it signals a bite from a fish by dancing in the water. Most bobbers sold today are made of plastic, and they attach to the line by a spring loaded clip that allows easy movement of the bobber up and down the line.

The main disadvantage of a bobber is that it provides resistance when a fish mouths the bait, often enough to make the fish reject it. Therefore, it is important to use a bobber that will produce as little "drag" on the bait as possible. In earlier years, a wooden bobber shaped like a slender diamond was widely used; being slim, it did not offer much resistance to a biting fish. But, because it was long and took up a lot of space in the tackle box, it declined in popularity and was quickly displaced when the plastic models came on the market. If you do a lot of bobber fishing, though, you might want to locate or make one of these slender bobbers.

Most of the bobbers you'll see in the stores today are round or teardrop shaped. The round ones float high and are easy to see, but they offer the greater resistance to the fish. If you use a round bobber, select one as small as possible. The teardrop types are less troublesome as far as drag is concerned, but they are harder to see, especially in water that has some surface disturbance.

Traditional bobber colors are red and white, and most old-timers prefer those colors, but nowadays you can get bobbers in glowing fluorescent colors. If you can stand to look at them at all, you'll find them easy to see, especially in poor light.

Another tip: select a bobber that has two positions for the clip, one to tightly squeeze the line and one that allows the line to pass through **19** the clip freely. This second feature is needed in situations where you need to suspend the bait several feet below the bobber. If you were to clip the bobber tight to the line at, say, four feet from the bait, you'd have a difficult time casting because the line couldn't be reeled in any further than the bobber allowed. But if you make a loop in the line at the selected distance from the bait and insert a rubber band in the loop, then clip the bobber between that point and the bait with the clip set in the open position, the bobber will slide right down to the bait when you cast. It will sit on top of the water and let the line slide through until the rubber band snugs up against the bobber, suspending the bait at your preferred level.

Swivels

Swivels are used to help keep lures that spin from twisting the monofilament fishing line. They also keep line resistance from interfering with the action of such lures. Since monofilament tends to kink with lures of many different actions and since it may also twist when the angler reels in an unstable bait that revolves in the water, swivels are used often in freshwater fishing. There are three main types: snap, barrel, and three-way.

SNAP SWIVEL

The snap swivel consists of a round swivel with an eye on one end to which the line is attached and a safety pin type snap on the other to which the lure or baited hook is attached. In addition to eliminating line twist, snap swivels make it easy to change bait and lures frequently without tying new knots each time.

Snap swivels are available in a wide range of sizes. Your dealer can make a recommendation on the size most suited to your line and most frequently used lures. Since these swivels are not expensive, it's a good idea to carry a selection of several sizes with you all the time. You must also consider whether you want the bright, plated swivels or the black or brown, dull-finished kind. Some anglers think that bright swivels add additional flash to lures; others think they detract from them. Occasionally, game fish will strike at a bright swivel instead of the lure. In that case, you'll want to have some dull-finished ones along to switch to.

Finally, keep in mind that snap swivels can interfere with the action of some lures, particularly surface plugs. If the lure you're using does not spin in revolutions, you can probably use it without a swivel without twisting your line. Experiment to see if the action is better when the lure is tied directly to your line.

BARREL SWIVEL

The barrel swivel is an oval type with an eye at each end so that it is usually tied somewhere *in* the line rather than at the end of it. If you were trolling with fabric line, for example, you might want a leader of clear monofilament between the braided line and your lure. A barrel swivel between the fabric line and your "mono" leader would be the answer.

Sometimes spinner fishermen don't want a snap swivel right at their lure, yet they still need protection against line twist. In such a situation, a barrel swivel located a couple of feet from the point of lure attachment solves the problem. As indicated earlier, many ultralight anglers like to use a shock leader of a heavier test than their line. The barrel swivel provides a good method of linking line and leader.

THREE-WAY SWIVEL

A three-way swivel is most often used for bottom fishing. One eye attaches to the main fishing line, one to the sinker, and the third to the bait. This arrangement holds the bait off the bottom while allowing retrieve without the line twisting.

Keep in mind that all these little items can be used in unorthodox ways. One of the possible problems in bottom bait fishing, for example, is the sinker. You need the sinker to get the bait down to the fish, but once there it may provide so much resistance to a fish attempting to move away with the bait that the fish drops it before the angler can set the hook. Use a snap swivel and a dipsey to solve the problem. Before tying on the snap swivel that you will use to attach your baited hook, thread the line through the eye of a second snap swivel so that the swivel can move freely up and down the line. Then, once you've baited up, attach a dipsey to the snap of the free-running swivel and make your cast. When the fish picks up the bait, the sinker will sit on the bottom, and your line will flow freely through the eye of the snap swivel, eliminating most of the resistance.

When you assemble your supply of sinkers, swivels, and other small items, be sure to keep them separated and well organized. Small sinkers usually come in appropriate containers, but the larger ones are often bought loose and must be organized and stored by the angler. Plastic boxes with individual compartments are good storage containers. The old-type plastic pill containers with snap-on caps are ideal for swivels and hooks, if you can find them. The new ones with the "child-proof" lids are often nearly adult-proof, too; if you use them, be sure to reserve them for seldom-used items. A better solution is the plastic

21

container that 35mm film comes in. Neither the new pill bottles nor Kodak film containers are transparent, so you'll have to mark them on the outside to identify the contents. Fuji film, however, is sold in clear plastic containers.

Tackle Boxes

Like a lot of other subjects in fishing, the types of tackle boxes have recently become so numerous and so sophisticated that it's difficult to keep track of all the possibilities when the time comes to make your selection. On the other hand, anglers have never had such a wide selection as they have today.

As a beginner, you'll probably purchase a first tackle box that is on the small side. That's a good idea, because the larger ones have more specialized features, and you won't know which of those features will suit your fishing until you have more experience. If you buy a small box of good quality, your money won't be wasted, even if you do outgrow it later. You'll find a good use for it, perhaps to hold seldom-used tackle. Or perhaps you'll be one of those anglers who prefers several small boxes to one large one.

Most of today's quality tackle boxes are made of high-impact plastic rather than the metal that was once the sign of a high quality box. The plastic is durable, and it's lighter, quieter, and easier to fabricate into handy configurations than metal. Also, plastic is noncorrosive, an important feature in any product that's used around water.

There are several types of plastic boxes. Here's a rundown.

SATCHEL BOXES

Satchel boxes are made like small suitcases or briefcases. The sides are usually transparent plastic to reveal the lures and accessories in the trays underneath.

DRAWER BOXES

In the drawer box, a side panel is removed, and a series of drawers is revealed that pull out horizontally from the box. These boxes offer a lot of capacity for their size, because the whole box is devoted to storage space with little room taken up by cantilevers, hinges, and the like. Some of them offer additional drawers, so that the box can be packed with only the tackle you need for a particular trip. Some also have an "underbox" that can hold large items, such as reels, which are not suited to drawer storage.

FIGURE 2–4 Three styles of tackle box from Flambeau Plastics Corporation. *Clockwise from lower left:* a satchel–type box, a box with individual cartridges carried in a tray with storage area underneath, and a box with cantilevered trays and a special carrier for spinners. *Lower right:* a small plastic box for the wading angler. (Photo by David Guiney)

CARTRIDGE BOXES

The cartridge box is a variation on the drawer idea, except that it holds individual tackle boxes carried on a removable tray with a storage area underneath. As in the drawer boxes, additional small boxes can be purchased from the manufacturer, if you choose. A cartridge-type box is shown in Figure 2–4. Such boxes are ideal for the travelling angler and are good for carrying fly-tying materials, too.

TRUNK BOXES

Trunk boxes are made like the traditional metal tackle box. The lid opens to show a series of cantilevered trays. Under the trays is additional storage space.

HIP-ROOF BOXES

Boxes of the hip-roof type provide the most compartments for individual
23 lures, hooks, hardware, and such. With the lid open, trays cantilever in

one or both directions depending on the box. Well storage is available under the trays. Because this design lends itself to so many trays, the largest of the tackle boxes (and they are huge) are of hip-roof construction.

You'll probably want to look over several samples of these five types of boxes before you decide on the style of box that suits you best. While you're looking, you should also make sure that the boxes you're considering also have the basic elements of good quality, regardless of their design. Look for:

1. *Waterproof Design.* If you often plan to fish in real downpours, avoid boxes of the hip-roof type if they have an opening across the top where the seam is exposed to rain. And look for overlapping lips on all closure seams wherever they are. Also note the handle design; if it's attached by rivets or screws through the top of the box, there's a potential leak area, and it may have to be sealed with tub sealant. The type with the handle attachment molded as part of the box is better.

2. *Spill-Proof Design.* Look for a latch that will not come open until you open it. A spilled tackle box is a terrible mess whether you're coming or going.

3. *Corrosion-Resistant Hardware.* The metal fixtures on the box should be chrome-plated or stainless steel to resist corrosion in saltwater areas. Such hardware will also resist rusting and atmospheric deterioration wherever you live.

4. *Adjustable Compartments.* The best boxes offer compartments that can be modified by installing extra plastic dividers, provided with the box. As your needs grow and your fishing habits change, such versatility can help an old box keep up with your needs and save you the expense of buying a new one.

5. *Worm-Proof Trays.* The soft plastic used in artificial worms and other plastic baits will react chemically with ordinary hard plastic to eat right through it. Your box should have at least some compartments or trays designed specially to carry such lures.

6. *Strong Hinges.* Your box will be opened and closed thousands of times, and all-plastic hinges won't stand the strain. Look for hinges with metal pins that run the length of the box.

7. *Locking Capability.* Your box will contain tackle worth a lot of money, and you will be taking it on camping trips, leaving it in your car, leaving it in your boat while you wade. Being able to lock it provides some additional security—locking it *to* something is better yet.

8. *Stacking Capability.* You may own several tackle boxes eventu-

ally, and stacking them will make better use of your storage area. Look for flat tops and flush-folding handles.

Other
Tackle
Toters

A tackle box is fine for the boating angler or the person who sits down and "still fishes" at one place for a spell. But what about the wading angler, or backpacker, or the fellow who just likes to keep moving from one spot to another? For anglers like these, a tackle box is an encumbrance. A fishing vest is probably the answer.

VEST

The vest is so often associated with fly fishing that it is often called a "fly vest." But that's not so much because of the specialized nature of fly tackle as because the fly fisherman is always on the move. If you move around a lot in your fishing, the vest might be the answer for you, no matter what sort of tackle you prefer.

The fishing vest is basically a sleeveless shirt with many pockets. The pockets are designed to fit fly and lure boxes of standard size (more about them later). If you fish "on the move" only occasionally, an inexpensive vest will do nicely, but if you make this your regular method, you'll want a pretty good one. High quality vests show the following features:

FIGURE 2–5 A fishing vest and some of its contents (Photo by Katherine Lee)

25

1. Strong construction. Most of the good vests are made from a blend of polyester and cotton with double-stitched seams to carry the weight that accumulates in a vest. Avoid bright colors; they may alarm fish. Experienced anglers choose green or tan.

2. Zippers and Velcro closings. Since snaps require two hands to close, they are a constant annoyance. Velcro on small pockets is the answer—slap the pocket shut and it's secure. Larger pockets require zippers made of rustproof brass or nylon. You'll prefer zippers with large tabs because they're easier to grab without fumbling.

3. Plenty of room and specialized pockets for certain items. Good quality vests have pockets inside and out, and the larger pockets are "bellows" type so that they can accommodate extra boxes and other gear. Most have an extra-large, zippered pocket across the back for lunch, rain jacket, and other occasional gear. Special pockets for sunglasses, insect repellent, and such are handy.

Once you have such a vest, give some thought to how you organize it. Put your most frequently needed items in the front pockets, your less essential stuff on the inside. Consider inventing a system that will make the use of your vest automatic. For example, you might put all your floating lures and associated hardware on the right side, your sinking lures on the left. Your goal should be a storage system so comfortable and so well organized that you can reach for what you want without thinking.

HANDY ANDY

Some anglers prefer another sort of arrangement to the vest, one called the "Handy Andy." This is basically two small packs suspended from shoulder straps so that one pack hangs on your chest, the other down your back. You get to the back pack by simply turning the whole arrangement around.

The twin-pack setup does not lend itself to precise organization like the vest does, but then maybe you won't carry so much stuff that you need a precise system with a separate pocket for everything. And, if you carry a lot of bulky items that don't lend themselves to pocket transport, the Handy Andy is for you. Since it distributes the weight of your load a little more evenly than the vest, you may find the Handy Andy more comfortable. See Figure 2–6.

FISHING BAG

A final alternative to the vest is the fishing bag. Although a few fishermen have used homemade versions of this device for years, there are now a number of commercial bags on the market. The bag is suspended by a

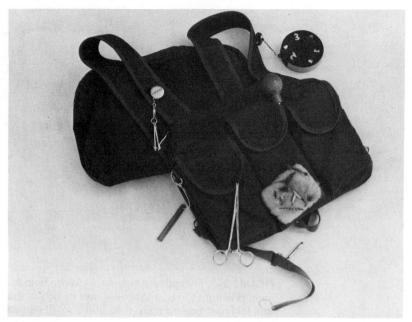

FIGURE 2–6 The chest-and-backpack alternative to the vest (Photo by Katherine Lee)

strap from one shoulder or around the neck and is carried on the hip until needed. The commercial versions of the fishing bag have pockets both inside and out.

Lure Boxes

Lure boxes are essential if you're going to fish with a vest, Handy Andy, or tackle bag, and most anglers use a few boxes for organization even in their tackle boxes. Most of the lure boxes you'll consider are plastic—it's lightweight, quiet, durable, and nonreflective. There are several different designs.

THE COMPARTMENT BOX

The compartment box has compartments of various sizes to hold lures, hooks, sinkers, and the like. These boxes are available in many different compartment configurations, and you're certain to find one that meets your needs. Most have either clear lids or are clear all the way through, making it easy to locate what you want before opening the lid. The heavy plastic boxes are the least expensive, but they are comparatively heavy and may react chemically with soft plastic lures. The lightweight plastic boxes are more expensive, but less bulky, and they also have metal

27

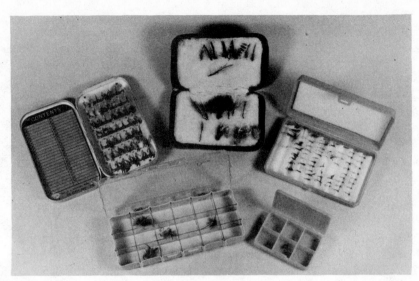

FIGURE 2–7 Fly and lure boxes. *Clockwise from lower left center:* a compartment box from Orvis, a Wheatley wet fly box, a sheepskin streamer book, the Ripple–Foam box from Fly–Rite, and a small compartment box from the same company. Although flies are shown here, all except the wet fly box can be used to carry other lures. (Photo by David Guiney)

hinges in most cases, making them far more durable than the heavy plastic boxes with plastic hinges.

The main disadvantage of compartment boxes is that lures and hooks tend to tangle in them, and a tangle of spinners with treble hooks, for example, is a tangle indeed. If you carry a lot of lures in boxes like this, one of the alternative designs might be better for your purpose.

THE SPINNER BOX

The spinner box is one way for the mobile angler to contend with the tangle problem. It holds spinners individually by the shaft of the treble hook so that several spinners can't tangle together. The system works, but the box does not have as large a capacity as other boxes of similar overall size. Nor does this box lend itself to carrying other types of lures or accessory hardware.

THE FOAM BOX

Boxes with plastic foam inserts for holding hooks were introduced **28** primarily for the benefit of fly fishermen, but they are useful for stream fishermen of all persuasions. The foam holds hooks securely, and tangles are avoided; with careful packing, the capacity of a foam box is somewhat greater than that of the spinner box. Foam boxes are more versatile, too; anything with hooks can be carried in a foam lure box. One of the most useful of the foam boxes is the Ripple-Foam box, shown in Figure 2–7. The raised portions of the foam make it easy to insert and withdraw hooks.

The one disadvantage of foam: if wet hooks are reinserted into it, they may rust. But a prudent angler dries hooks and lures before putting them back into any box.

Odds and Ends

Let's finish this chapter with a listing of little items that eventually find their way into most tackle boxes and fishing vests. Most are not absolutely essential . . . until you need them.

KNIFE

The Swiss Army knife is probably the most popular with fishermen. With the largest of these tool-filled weapons, you could probably fix your boat motor, erect an emergency shelter, or carve a totem pole. With the smaller versions, you can still clean and file your nails, pick your teeth, cut up bait, and use the scissors to cut articles out of your favorite fishing magazines.

If you like to eat fish as well as catch them, there are many knives available (including a couple of the Swiss Army types) that include fish scalers along with the other tools. And you'll probably want one of the whippet-thin fillet knives for cleaning and boning your catch.

RAIN SUIT

Inexpensive plastic rain suits, available at your local discount store, are fine for emergency use, and they fold into a small package that you can store in your boat or tackle box. Wading anglers can store the jacket in their vests; they don't need the pants.

If you fish in the rain intentionally (and that's a good idea), you'll be much more comfortable in one of the modern rain suits incorporating Gore-Tex or similar fabric. These garments will pass perspiration away from your body while keeping rain out. They are expensive, but unless you like to be miserable during warm-weather rainy spells, you may find they're worth the cost. See Figure 2–8 for a sample of rain clothing.

FIGURE 2–8 Two examples of Gore–Tex rain gear. *Left:* the author wearing Terrashell from Early Winters, Ltd. *Right:* David Guiney in lightweight Gore–Tex jacket from Chinook Sport, Ltd. (Photo by David Guiney)

SUNGLASSES

You want polarized sunglasses for fishing. They're designed to combat *reflected* glare, and that's what you face in fishing situations. They also enable you to look into the water and see obstructions, bottom features, and *fish.* Stream anglers in particular would be lost without their polarized glasses.

If you wear prescription glasses already, you can buy clip-ons, or you can order custom-made, prescription, polarized glasses through some opticians. Gray, green, blue, and tan lenses are available. Most anglers like tan or green.

WADING GEAR

If you're a stream fisherman, you'll need to get some hip boots or chest waders, depending on the depth of the water where you intend to wade.

Hip boots come with rubber lug soles or felt soles; although the felt soles wear more rapidly, they provide much better footing in the rocky streambeds that are typical haunts of the stream angler. Felt sole replacement kits are available at a reasonable cost.

If you decide you need waders, you have another decision to consider: boot foot or stocking foot. The boot foot waders come with either the lug soles or felt soles, just like the hip boots. Stocking foot waders require the addition of a wading shoe. While the wader-wading shoe combination is much more expensive than the boot foot wader, it's also much more comfortable and provides better traction. If you fish in waders a lot, the stocking foot type is probably the way to go. You then order wading shoes (almost all with felt soles) separately. Be sure to get your wading shoes a little bigger than usual, because you'll have a couple of pairs of heavy socks to pack inside, plus the stocking foot section of the waders.

HOOK DISGORGER

There are many commercial types of hook disgorgers, but the best of all is a pair of hemostats, or forceps. These lock around the hook, making dislodging easy. They can be purchased at your local medical supply store, or you can ask your doctor for a pair. The medium-sized curved ones are best.

INSECT REPELLENT

Bug repellent is available in stick, cream, liquid, or spray. The spray is wasteful, but easy to apply; the other types are economical, but in applying them you may get the stuff on your hands and, from there, on your lures, baits, and hooks. Many anglers believe that insect repellents repel fish as well as bugs. If you use one of the nonspray types, carry a bar of Ivory soap for washing your hands after application. And be aware that some insect repellents can damage plastic products, such as fly lines.

HOOK HONE

Most tackle shops carry these, usually the flat ones with a slot on one side for inserting the hook point. You might also need a needle point hook hone for sharpening small hooks and a file for sharpening large ones. If you want to go all out, battery-powered hook hones are now available.

HAT

A hat with some sort of brim is desirable. It will keep rain out of your eyes and gnats, as well, since they won't fly into the shade. Particularly good is the long-billed fishing hat with an extra bill in back to be pulled down to protect the angler's neck from sunburn. The bill of any fishing hat should be green underneath to help cut glare coming off the water. Waterproof hats of Gore-Tex are available too, and you might consider one if you like to fish in the rain.

FIRST AID KIT

Choose your kit based on your carrying capacity and the distance you expect to be from medical help should an emergency arise.

DRINKING CUP

If you take a drinking cup, take some water purification tablets, too.

FINGERNAIL CLIPPERS

The best thing for clipping monofilament cleanly and accurately is fingernail clippers. You'll use these so often that they should be carried on your person, ideally on one of the little pin-on reels that will retract them after use. A short length of fly line makes for a good attachment, too.

LIGHT

You'll probably carry a small disposable flashlight in your tackle box. You might want to consider one of the new lithium-cell flashlights. They're expensive, but the batteries last about ten years in ordinary use.

If you're a wading fisherman, you might want one of the small lights that clips to your shirt or hangs around your neck on a cord. These make it easy to change lures and tie knots after dark.

LANDING NET

A landing net is often essential in landing a good fish, especially from a boat. For boat use, you'll want the long-handled aluminum type. For stream use the short-handled net is better, and you can keep it out of the way by hanging it from your belt or the back of your vest on one of the chain retractors designed for holding rings of keys. You'll find these in hardware stores.

TAPE MEASURE

If you fish from a boat, you can tape a plastic tape measure to the seat or floor and avoid the need to carry anything. If you fish streams, you can mark your rod at a known distance from the handle and "guesstimate" from there. Or you can buy one of the little gadgets that has a tape measure and a scale for weighing your fish. One caution—these scales may injure fish, so don't use them on fish you intend to release.

CREEL

For a wading fisherman who wants some fish for the pan, a creel is necessary. The old-fashioned split willow type works as well as ever, and the new types work by the principle of evaporation. Boat anglers usually put fish in the live well, or in the cooler, which most just happen to have along . . .

THERMOMETER

If you find you're a record-keeping angler, water temperature is a piece of data that you'll need. Temperature is a critical factor in the activity of fish and of the underwater organisms that they feed on. It's a good idea to take the temperature several times a day, record the reading and the location, and note fishing action at that time and place.

The best thermometer is the type aquatic biologists use. It's protected by a metal or plastic tube, has a pocket clip as well as a ring for attaching a safety line.

Now, at long last, we're ready to begin talking about the equipment that you probably thought we'd start with: rods and reels. Hopefully, this information about terminal tackle and accessories has given you a better idea of the things you need to keep in mind when selecting your casting tackle.

CHAPTER **3**

Spinning

Spinning is a method of casting in which the lure is cast from an open, fixed-spool reel mounted under the rod. The spool is mounted parallel to the rod and does not revolve, but allows line to follow the lure by peeling off the forward end in loops. Because the spool does not revolve, spinning equipment eliminates the major cause of backlashes.

Spinning tackle was first available in this country in the mid-1930s, but World War II intervened before the method became widely known here. During the war, many American servicemen became familiar with the technique (which had originated in Europe), and when the war ended, spinning rapidly became a favorite method of freshwater angling in America.

The rapid popularity of spinning was in part due to the deficiencies of the revolving-spool bait-casting tackle of the post-war period. That equipment was so often subject to backlashes that anglers cursed their tackle as often as they enjoyed it. And since the heavy casting reels of the day required heavy lures or baits to set the spool in motion, the light lure capability of the spinning outfit made a whole new kind of fishing available to American fishermen.

If you refer to the illustration of a spinning reel in Figure 3–1, you'll see why the method offers so many advantages. The reel, remember, is designed to be mounted under the rod handle. The *reel spool* faces toward the front of the rod and is angled slightly up. For best casting, the spool is filled (usually with monofilament) to within about one-eighth inch of the lip of the spool. When the *reel handle* is first turned following the cast, the *bail* closes over the spool (it will be opened before another cast is made) and winds the line back on again. As the bail is turning, gears within the *gear housing* move the spool in and out so that the line is evenly spooled instead of piling up at one point.

Above the housing is the *reel foot*, which attaches to the rod handle. At the back or top of the housing is the *antireverse* lever or switch. When this is engaged, neither the reel handle nor the bail will turn backwards; if line is to be taken off the reel, it must be pulled off against the resistance of the *drag*. On most reels, the drag is adjusted with the *brake screw*, which also holds the spool on the reel. On some spinning reels, the drag adjustment is located at the rear of the housing rather than in front of the spool.

Behind the spool is the *cup*, which holds the internal parts of the bail. Most modern reels feature skirted spools that overlap the cup, eliminating a crack between the cup and spool that sometimes traps the line and also can allow dirt to enter the innards of the reel.

Now check the rod on which the spinning reel is mounted. See

FIGURE 3–1 A typical spinning rod and reel

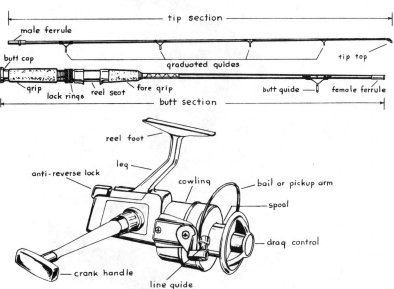

35

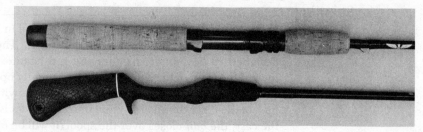

FIGURE 3–2 Fenwick graphite rods. *Top:* On the spinning rod, the reel is mounted under the rod. *Bottom:* On the casting rod, the reel goes on top. (Photo by David Guiney)

Figures 3–2 and 3–3 for a comparison between spinning and casting rods. Note that the spinning rod has a straight *hand grip* with fixtures for mounting the reel below the grip. Note too that the *guides* on the spinning rod are much larger than those on the casting rod and are mounted on the underside of the rod blank. If you look closely at Figure 3–1, you'll note that the guides on the spinning rod that are closest to the reel are the largest and that they gradually become smaller toward the

FIGURE 3–3 The first guide. *Top:* a spinning rod. *Bottom:* a casting rod. The rods are the Fenwicks shown in the previous illustration. (Photo by David Guiney)

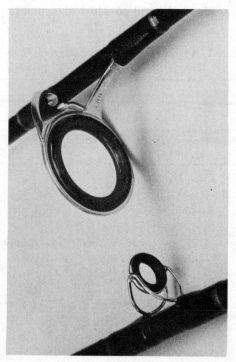

tip of the rod, forming a funnel shape for the line to pass through. This is necessary because the line loops off the spinning reel in large spirals, which must be gradually choked down into a straight line by the time the line leaves the rod.

Spinning tackle is easy to use. As the line leaves the spool during the lure's flight, the amount of line on the spool diminishes, which results in increased friction between the line loops and the spool lip, which in turn slows the release of the line. The lure begins its journey at high speed and then slows continuously until it falls on the water. This harmony between the physics of lure flight and the release of line from the reel makes spinning a trouble-free form of casting.

Another advantage of spinning gear is that it is less costly than bait-casting tackle of comparable quality; at least the reels can be, because they are simpler and don't require the precise tolerances of good quality bait-casting reels. And most spinning anglers like the fact that they retrieve line by winding with their left hand (although the handle is reversible on most reels now). The left hand retrieve eliminates changing the rod from hand to hand; the right hand casts the rod and plays the fish while the left hand retrieves line as necessary. And you'll probably like the spinning configuration of the reel under the rod. It's very comfortable once you get used to it, especially if you often fish for long periods at a time.

Spinning, however, is not ideal for all fishing situations. Spinning tackle is not well suited to fishing surface plugs, because the manipulation of these plugs creates slack line that the spinning reel does not respool very evenly. And many bait fishermen, especially those who enjoy still fishing, don't like spinning gear because the location of the reel makes it inconvenient to finger the line to detect nibbles. Most jig artists and plastic worm anglers prefer heavier bait-casting equipment for their fishing, especially when they're fishing over and through a lot of obstructions.

You should consider spinning tackle if:

1. You expect to do a lot of fishing with underwater artificial lures, especially spinners and spoons.
2. You will fish often with soft, natural baits that weigh little.
3. You expect to do most of your fishing with lures at the lighter end of the spectrum and with line of eight pound test or less.
4. You are interested in ultralight fishing.

Spinning tackle comes in many different lengths, weights, and actions. The manufacturers do not always agree on their terminology, and that's a problem for the beginner. What one maker calls a "light" action rod might be designated "medium" by another. Table 3–1 will help you sort it out to some degree. Note that in the "light" and "medium" categories, the difference is not in the size of the rods, but in the action. This should alert you to the fact that you should select your outfit based on the line and lure weights you intend to cast; *then* shop around for your other preferences, such as length, one-piece or two-piece rod blank, and so on. You'll also see that there is considerable overlap between categories. By selecting your tackle carefully and adding a couple of extra reel spools filled with lines of different tests, you can cover a wide range of lure sizes with only one outfit.

TABLE 3–1
Spinning Tackle

Designation	Rod Length	Rod Weight	Test Line	Lure Weight
Ultralight	4$^1/_2$–6 ft.	1$^1/_2$–3$^1/_2$ oz.	1–4 lb.	$^1/_{16}$–$^5/_{16}$ oz.
Light	5–7$^1/_2$ ft.	4–7 oz.	4–10 lb.	$^1/_8$–$^1/_2$ oz.
Medium	6–7$^1/_2$ ft.	5–7 oz.	6–14 lb.	$^1/_8$–1 oz.
Heavy	6$^1/_2$–8 ft.	6–8 oz.	8–20 lb.	$^1/_4$–1 oz.

FIGURE 3–4 Two approaches to light spinning. *Bottom:* a light–action Sigma outfit from Shakespeare. *Top:* an ultra–light combo from Garcia. Note the lightweight handle and sliding reel bands on the ultra–light gear. (Photo by David Guiney)

FIGURE 3–5 The new "Fast Cast" rig from Shimano. The same finger that catches the line lifts a trigger that opens the bail, making casting a one-hand operation. (Photo by David Guiney)

Most beginners are well satisfied with a first spinning outfit that features a rod of six to seven feet in length with a light action. A light reel that will spool two hundred yards of six-pound test line will match such a rod nicely, and you can add extra spools with four- and eight-pound line to cover most situations. Start with a good fiberglass rod from a reliable manufacturer and a reel either made to match it by the same maker or one recommended by your dealer. Rods of boron and graphite are available, and dandy, too, but you should start with a serviceable, less expensive rod. Then, if you really get interested in spinning, you'll buy that more expensive tackle with the experience you need to get exactly what you require.

Casting with Spinning Tackle

Spinning tackle is among the easiest to learn to cast with. Most beginners can achieve acceptable distance and accuracy with only an hour or so of practice. Be sure to buy a "practice plug" when you get your spinning outfit, one that weighs about the same as the lures you expect to cast most often. With the practice plug, you can get solid practice right in your own back yard.

39

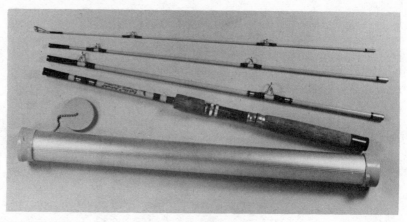

FIGURE 3–6 A spinning rod for backpackers from Eagle Claw. The rod converts to a fly rod by reversing the handle. (Photo by David Guiney)

BASIC SPINNING

When you grip a spinning rod, put two fingers in front of the reel foot leg and two behind. This balances the outfit nicely in your hand and puts the line within reach of your index finger. To begin the cast, wind the practice plug up to within a few inches of the rod tip, stopping when the bail line guide is on top of the spool. With the index finger of your rod hand, reach down and pick up the line. Many anglers like to hold the line in the crack under the first knuckle on that finger, but I prefer to hold the line further out toward the tip because it comes off the finger better in casting. Try it both ways and see which suits you better.

When the line is securely held on your finger, you are ready to open the bail and make your cast. Open the bail with your left hand; if you forget to do this (as you will occasionally at first), your cast will go nowhere, because the line can't come off the spool.

In preparation for the cast, your body should be positioned as in Figure 3–7; you're angled slightly toward your target, your elbows are close to, but not touching, your body, and your forearm is in line with the rod.

As in the other casting illustrations in this book, an imaginary clock face governs the casting movements. The clock face is beside you, and, as the illustration shows, your rod tip should be aimed at the target and held at about the ten o'clock position.

To begin the cast, lift the rod swiftly to about the one o'clock position, not with the whole arm, but by pivoting at the elbow. As Figure 3–7 shows, the power stroke on this "back cast" ends at one o'clock. As the rod slows and stops, the weight of the lure bends or

40

FIGURE 3–7 Casting with spinning tackle (Illustration courtesy Zebco/Brunswick)

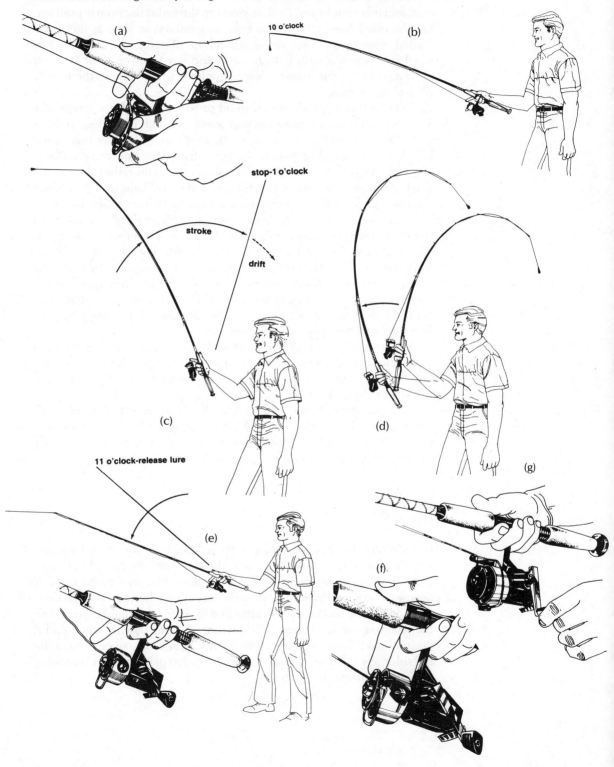

"loads" the rod as shown in Figure 3–7. This loading is essential to the cast, and it cannot happen unless you stop the rod at the proper position. On the other hand, the stop is only momentary; as soon as the rod is loaded, your forward stroke begins. As the illustration shows, the forward cast is made with both forearm and wrist power. And at about eleven o'clock, your finger releases the line, which follows the lure or plug to the target.

This eleven o'clock release point provides a satisfactory trajectory for most casts. If you find your cast going too high (including straight up!), you released the line too early. If your cast goes lower than you'd like (like landing right at your feet!), you released the line too late. This is one reason I prefer holding the line on my fingertip rather than in the crack of the knuckle; sometimes the line will sort of hang up in that crack (especially if your fingers are not smooth) and will be released too late.

As soon as the line is released, your line finger should drop toward the spool, ready to brake, or "feather," the line as it comes off the spool. This finger can slow the flight of the lure by controlling the release of line from the spool; in fact, you can stop the lure altogether by clamping down hard with the finger. One of the advantages of spinning is the ease with which you can control the lure's flight. You should practice this control right from the beginning and develop the habit of dropping your line finger to the spool lip on every cast.

When the lure makes contact with the water, your finger should touch the spool if it hasn't already done so. This touch will keep excess line from tumbling off the spool and prevent the buildup of slack line when you begin the retrieve.

As you begin to retrieve the line, the bail will automatically click into place and wind the line back on the spool again. When you have wound the plug back to within a few inches of the rod tip, you are ready to cast again. Don't forget to open the bail!

SIDE CAST

In addition to the basic spinning cast just described, you should practice several others. One easy variation is the side cast, illustrated in Figure 3–8. This cast is needed where obstructions like tree limbs make it necessary to send the lure toward the target on a horizontal trajectory. As you see, the motions are exactly like those for the standard cast, but the whole operation is now in a horizontal plane. Usually you'll find it desirable to release the line a little earlier than usual, since driving the rod sideways will tend to send the lure to the left of your target (assuming you're a right-handed caster).

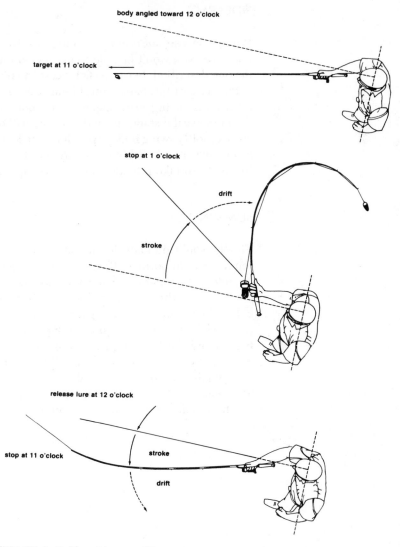

FIGURE 3–8 The side cast (Illustration courtesy Zebco/Brunswick)

UNDERHAND FLIP

Another basic cast is the underhand flip. This is a little like tossing a softball underhand; you drop the rod tip slightly and then flip it up, releasing line as the tip springs upward. You can't toss a lure very far with this technique, but then you don't need to. It's a cast for close-in fishing where the side cast would be too hard.

43

SIDEARM

When you use your spinning outfit to fish soft baits like worms and minnows, you won't be able to use a vigorous, wrist-snapping cast like the one described, because such a cast will flip the bait off nine times out of ten. To cast soft baits, you should make a sidearm, lob cast with your full arm, reducing wrist snap to almost nothing. Lowering the bait more than the usual distance from the rod tip will help in such a cast, because you can softly swing it like a pendulum to load the rod. The spinning rod is ideally suited to fishing soft and light baits, but you'll have to learn a soft pitch to take full advantage of its capabilities.

SUMMING UP

Finally, you'll gradually learn that the distance between rod tip and lure can have an important effect on the cast, both in terms of distance and trajectory. In general, a heavy lure casts best when reeled up to within a few inches of the tip; a light lure does better if allowed to hang further below the rod tip. Once you get the feel of spinning gear, you'll discover that each lure you cast requires a slight adjustment in distance between the tip and the lure to give optimal performance.

As with the other tackle you'll accumulate, you'll do best to stick with quality brands like those illustrated in this book. You may invest a little more initially, but your money will be well spent in terms of reliability and long life in your equipment. Happy spinning!

CHAPTER **4**

Bait Casting

Like many other anglers, I was taught to fish by my father. We fished for crappie and smallmouth bass, and I remember, not too fondly, the tackle we used. It was the bait-casting equipment of post-World War II when glass rods were still new (and not very good) and casting reels were still old (and in the hands of novices like me, not very good).

I can recall the casting process vividly. Dropping my lure or bait about four inches below the rod tip, I would place my thumb carefully on the revolving spool of the reel, just as my Dad and other experts did. Whipping the rod into a backcast stroke, I would power it forward, lifting my thumb when the reel came past my ear. Out the bait would fly, rocketing toward the target with a great whir of revolving reel handles. Then, suddenly, in midflight, the bait would stop stark still and fall with a splash far short of the target. And I would begin another ten- or fifteen-minute ordeal—unravelling the dreaded backlash.

In a way, it's too bad that modern bait-casting tackle has reduced backlashes to a minimum. Backlashes build character—I have no doubt. Trying to pick them free certainly engenders patience, and we all know that patience is one of the cardinal virtues of the angler. And certainly backlashes are desirable from a conservation standpoint. One of the reasons that catch-and-release fishing was unknown when I was a boy was that fishermen fooling with snarled reels didn't catch any fish and thus had no need to release them!

To be sure, backlashes have not disappeared entirely. You can still have one if you insist, even with today's sophisticated casting gear. But they are much less common than they used to be; they're just frequent enough now to focus your attention on how to avoid them. In the hands of a skilled angler, today's bait-casting tackle will do all the good things it could do in my childhood—and more.

Bait-Casting Tackle

The ancestor of the modern bait-casting reel (or plug-casting, as it is often called today) was invented by George Snyder of Kentucky in 1810. The essence of that early reel was multiplication: Snyder's reel took in several turns of line on the spool for each single turn of the reel handle. Such a reel could be made smaller and could hold much more line than a single-action reel.

The first major improvement in the casting reel came when the level-wind feature was added later in the nineteenth century. This was a line guide that moved back and forth across in front of the spool, guiding the line evenly on the spool. The guide reduced line snarls from uneven spooling and made longer casts possible, because the line came off the spool more evenly.

From the beginning though, backlashes were the bane of the bait-casting reel. Backlashes are line snarls caused by spool overrun; in other words, the line keeps peeling off the spool after the lure has already stopped or slowed down and wraps itself into a mess around the reel spool.

Backlashes happen because the principles of lure flight and of spool rotation are in conflict. When a lure or bait is thrown through the air, its greatest momentum is at the beginning of its flight, and it is continually slowed down thereafter by the resistance of the air in front and the drag of the line behind. However, the reel spool tends to revolve more rapidly as the lure flies out instead of slowing down. If you've watched a movie projector closely, you've noted that as the amount of film on the spool diminishes, the spool turns faster and faster. The same thing happens on a bait-casting reel, and, if unchecked, a backlash will result every time.

Until recently, the only protection against backlashes was the "educated thumb." The angler applied thumb pressure to the spool as the lure was cast, gradually slowing the spool's revolutions as the lure slowed down in the air. This method is still the expert's technique, but it is easier to apply to today's reels. And modern reels have some novel methods of reducing backlashes, especially for the beginner whose thumb still has a lot of learning to do.

One of the most important changes in modern reels is reduced spool mass and weight. Spool overrunning is in part a result of centrifugal force; therefore, anything that reduces the weight of the revolving spool reduces overrunning to a degree. Most reels now also have a "free spool" button as well, which disengages the reel handles during the cast, eliminating still more rotating mass. And, since today's reel spools are so light, light lures and soft casts can start them turning; the old time reels were so heavy that they had to be jerked into rotation, and only heavy lures and baits could do that.

Casting, then, is more delicate, and fewer backlashes make the whole process much more satisfying. Most important, modern casting reels have internal spool brakes that automatically slow down the revolving spool as the line goes out. These brakes are adjusted according to the weight of the lure or bait being cast, and they apply a predetermined amount of drag to the spool. Because most of these brakes reduce the absolute distance and accuracy of the cast, experts generally ignore them or even remove them from their reels. For the beginner, however, they are a godsend.

Don't get the idea that you have nothing special to do when casting one of the modern outfits. Casting with bait-casting tackle is still a much more skilled operation than casting with spinning or spin-casting gear. You'll still need to use your thumb to some degree to control the spool, and as it becomes more "educated," you'll rely on it more and more. But with today's casting tackle, you'll have far fewer problems in the beginning and many fewer backlashes over the course of your fishing than the old-timers did, even the experts.

Take a glance at Figure 4–1 to see the main parts of a modern bait-casting reel. The *reel foot* is under the reel and mounts on top of the

FIGURE 4–1 A modern bait-casting reel

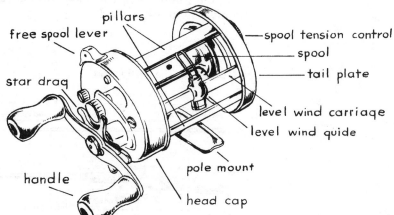

pillars

free spool lever

spool tension control

spool

tail plate

star drag

level wind carriage

level wind guide

handle

pole mount

head cap

rod. The *handle* is either a single finger grip with a counterweight or a traditional double handle. On most reels, the *drag control* is mounted on the handle shaft, usually of the *star drag* type as shown. Somewhere toward the rear of the reel, where the angler's thumb can reach it easily, is the *free-spool* mechanism, either a lever or a button, which disengages the handles during casting. The body of the reel on the handle side is called the *head cap* and is a cover for the internal parts of the reel, mostly gears, on the handle side. On some reels, the head cap screws right off, like the cap of a bottle. On others, a couple of screws have to be removed to get at the innards. On the other side of the reel is the *tail plate*, which covers the internal parts on the nonhandle side. On many reels, the tail plate is rounded and smooth to make "palming" the reel more comfortable. Most reels have the *spool tension control*, or *casting brake*, in the center of the tail plate, usually in the form of a knurled knob. Separating the head cap and tail plate are the *reel pillars*, on one of which rides the *level-wind guide*. In the center, of course, is the reel *spool* itself.

The rod on which such a reel is mounted is illustrated in Figure 4–2. On practically all modern casting rods (and these same rods are used in spin-casting discussed later), the *reel seat* is offset with a *reel lock* to secure the reel. Most *hand grips* are now of synthetic material, usually in the pistol grip style shown. In a casting rod, the *guides* are on top, and they are smaller than on a spinning rod, because the line comes off a casting reel relatively straight and does not have to be choked down as it does when peeling off a spinning reel.

At one time, braided line was used almost exclusively on casting reels, but that is no longer the case. Monofilament is probably the most commonly used now, except with anglers who troll with casting gear and want the lesser stretch of braided fabric line. As with other types of tackle, the line must be selected based on the weight of the lures or bait to be cast. Ten-pound test is probably typical for most casting applications, but where big fish or heavy cover are anticipated, line as heavy as twenty-pound test is used.

FIGURE 4–2 The casting rod

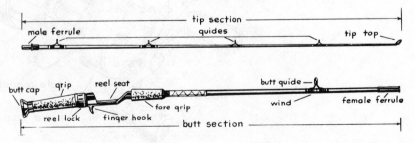

The bait-casting gear of my childhood was suitable for only fairly heavy fishing, because heavy lures were required to get the spool revolving. But the advances that have reduced backlashes have made casting equipment more versatile, too. Many good light casting reels will handle six-pound line and lures as light as three-sixteenths ounce. And some casting-tackle buffs who want to fish ultralight customize their light reels to handle four-pound and even two-pound line and one-eighth ounce lures. They put tooth paste in the gears and fish with the reel for a day or so (the abrasives in the tooth paste smooth out the mechanism). Then they clean the reel meticulously, remove all unneeded parts, lubricate it with the lightest of oils, and go fishing. This, of course, is specialized stuff, for experts only, but it gives a good idea of just how drastically casting tackle has been transformed by the changes of the last decade. If you're serious about ultralight fishing, stick with spinning tackle, at least at the start. Still, the average angler can expect to handle six-pound line and corresponding lures with suitably selected casting tackle.

Table 4–1 will give you a handle on the ranges of casting tackle in which you might be interested. Keep in mind that the table is an approximation; manufacturers have not fully agreed on what precisely constitutes "ultralight," "light," and so on. Also note that once you leave

FIGURE 4–3 The beautiful "Prolite" from Daiwa. This is one reel capable of casting 6-pound line and even lighter. (Photo by David Guiney)

the ultralight category, the length and weight of the rod are no longer reliable guides to the service to be expected from it. Most makers will describe their own interpretation of the action of the rod, and usually this information is written on the blank, just above the hand grip. Be prepared to look for a knowledgeable salesperson; these days many of them know less about fishing tackle than you do, especially those who work in discount stores. You will pay a little more by dealing with a reputable tackle shop, but the improved advice you get from the folks who work there will probably make it a good bargain.

TABLE 4–1
Bait-Casting Tackle

Designation	Rod Length	Rod Weight	Line	Lure Weight
Ultralight	$4\frac{1}{2}$–$5\frac{1}{2}$ ft.	1–$1\frac{1}{4}$ oz.	2–6 lb.	$\frac{1}{8}$–$\frac{3}{8}$ oz.
Light	5–6 ft.	$1\frac{1}{2}$–2 oz.	6–12 lb.	$\frac{1}{4}$–$\frac{5}{16}$ oz.
Medium	5–6 ft.	$1\frac{1}{2}$–2 oz.	8–18 lb.	$\frac{1}{4}$–$\frac{3}{4}$ oz.
Heavy	5–6 ft.	$1\frac{3}{4}$–$2\frac{1}{2}$ oz.	10–25 lb.	$\frac{3}{8}$–$1\frac{1}{2}$ oz.

Another good source of information about tackle is the catalogs of the prominent manufacturers, such as Shakespeare, Fenwick, Daiwa, Heddon, Eagle Claw, Zebco, and others. Some tackle shops carry these

FIGURE 4–4 Two high-quality casting outfits. *Top:* Sigma combination from Shakespeare. *Bottom:* "Striper" combo from Garcia. (Photo by David Guiney)

catalogs in stock, or you can get them from the makers either free or for a modest fee.

As a general rule, most beginners are well advised to learn about fishing with spin-casting or spinning tackle before graduating to bait-casting gear. Still, you might consider starting with bait-casting equipment if:

1. You live near good largemouth bass fishing and want to fish with plastic worms.
2. You want to fish for muskellunge or other large fish that require big lures.
3. You want or need to develop real pinpoint accuracy in casting.
4. You expect to do a lot of trolling.
5. You enjoy the challenge of mastering sophisticated and sometimes temperamental equipment.

If any of these situations applies to you, evaluate them in light of the chart. If you want a casting outfit for all-purpose use, you won't go far wrong with one in the light category, around five and a half feet in length with a good modern reel spooled with eight- or ten-pound monofilament. And once you get such an outfit, you'll need to learn how to use it.

Casting with Bait-Casting Tackle

You'll need lots of practice in casting with bait-casting tackle. Buy a practice plug in the same weight as the lures or bait that you intend to cast most often. Begin preparing for the cast by gripping the rod with your index finger over the trigger on the hand grip, your thumb securely on the reel spool. Release the free-spool lever or button with your other hand and tighten the casting brake knob all the way. Now, hold the rod level, take your thumb off the spool, and gradually loosen the brake knob until the practice plug falls slowly to the ground. This is the basic adjustment you make before casting with any lure, and you will need to readjust as you change to a lure of a different weight. If you are casting into a headwind that will slow the flight of the lure more rapidly than usual, set the tension a little tighter than you would otherwise. Using the brake like this will cut into your casting distance a little, but you shouldn't be concerned about distance in the beginning anyway, and the brake tension will provide protection against backlashes.

Once the spool brake is adjusted, you're ready to make your cast. Hold the rod as shown in Figure 4–5 with the handles pointing up. The reel is in free-spool, remember, and your thumb is resting on the spool. Take a position with your body at a slight angle to the target, and raise the rod until the tip is pointed at your target and at about the ten o'clock position on an imaginery clock face beside you. Start the cast with a swift movement of the rod up to a vertical position and just a bit beyond, stopping the rod firmly at the one o'clock position. Here the rod will be "loaded" by the weight of the lure swinging to the rear. See Figure 4–5 for a visual representation of the cast at this point.

Although you stop the rod fully on the back stroke, you begin the forward cast immediately; the two casting motions really blend into one. As you bring the rod forward, gently ease off the thumb pressure. The lure will take flight, and the spool will turn as it does while you provide subtle braking action with your thumb. Follow through on the cast by lowering the rod tip to follow the lure's flight, increasing thumb pressure again as the lure nears the target. When the lure lands, stop the spool rotation immediately by clamping down hard with your thumb. Switch hands to begin the retrieve, and begin winding with your casting hand. "Palming" the reel with your line hand, as shown in Figure 4–5g, allows much better control of the line and is essential when working a live bait or a plastic worm. Get in the habit of palming the reel from the beginning.

SIDE CAST

Once you have the feel of the overhead cast, practice the same cast in a horizontal plane. Such a side cast is needed when you have to drive your lure or bait back under some overhanging obstacle. It will take a while to get the hang of the side cast; for most casters, the side cast requires more wrist action and less forearm power than the overhead cast.

Once you've become proficient with bait-casting gear, you'll be able to take advantage of the unique capabilities that this tackle affords. If you decide to work with light-action tackle, you will learn to achieve accuracy that most spinning anglers only dream about. In the medium ranges, you'll get into worm-fishing for largemouth bass, working deep for stripers or walleyes, or fishing topwater plugs with guile and finesse. And if you decide to become a musky hunter, a heavy casting outfit will provide you with the power to toss the big plugs and live baits these fish respond to and to control the savage fight one of these bruisers can put up. And at whatever level, your "educated" thumb will prove your status as an expert angler.

FIGURE 4–5 Casting with bait-casting tackle (Illustration courtesy Zebco/Brunswick)

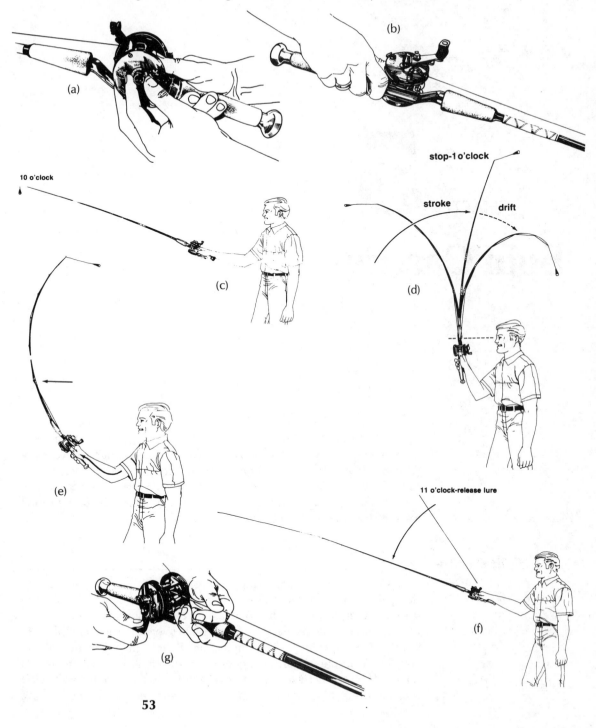

(a)

(b)

10 o'clock

stop-1 o'clock

stroke   drift

(c)

(d)

(e)

11 o'clock-release lure

(g)

(f)

5

Spin Casting

Spin-casting tackle is the most recently developed gear for the angler, but it has rapidly become the most popular in terms of sales. Spin casting (also known as closed-face spinning) represents a compromise between the spinning tackle and casting gear discussed in earlier chapters. While it has some limitations, it is such a fuss-free and generally easy form of casting that it appeals to anglers of all ages.

Spin-Casting Tackle

Like the spinning reel, the spin-casting reel utilizes a fixed spool with the line coming off one end of the spool during the cast. Unlike the spinning reel, however, the spin-casting reel is mounted on top of the rod and has a metal or plastic housing that covers the spool completely, allowing the line to pass through a small hole in the center of the housing. The spin-casting reel does not have a bail. Instead, the line is released for casting by the operation of a thumb button on the back of the reel and is taken up again by a metal or ceramic pin inside the housing

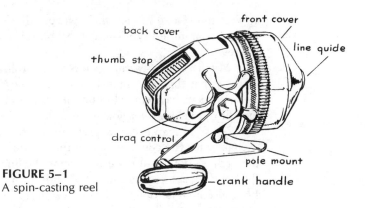

back cover

front cover

thumb stop

line guide

draq control

pole mount

crank handle

FIGURE 5–1
A spin-casting reel

that picks up the line and spools it when the handle is turned. Nothing could be simpler. If you can push a button and wind a handle, you can fish with spin-casting tackle. See Figure 5–1 for an illustration.

Spin-casting reels are designed to be mounted on standard casting rods, exactly the same as those described in the chapter on bait-casting. In fact, many anglers who like both techniques use only one rod and change reels when they move from one technique to the other.

A few closed-face reels are designed to be mounted under the rod like a standard spinning reel, and these require spinning rods for their

FIGURE 5–2 "Closed-Face Spinning" from Zebco. The reel mounts under a standard spinning rod, but the operation is like spin casting, except a finger trigger is substituted for the button on the top-mounted reel. (Photo by David Guiney)

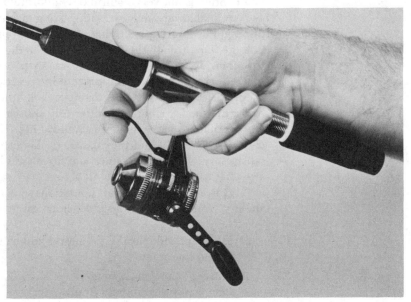

application. Once mounted, however, they work like the more common, top-mounted type—push the button to cast, wind the handle to retrieve.

All in all, spin-casting gear is an admirable compromise, and it's no wonder that this tackle has become the most common weapon on the water. It does have some limitations, although they might not be important in the fishing that you plan to do.

First, the spin caster gives up a little distance and accuracy in exchange for the convenience of the system. Distance is lost, because the high friction resulting from forcing the line through the small hole in the hood cuts efficiency compared with spinning and bait-casting tackle. For most anglers, this sacrifice in distance is not important, because the difference is small in the line weights and lure sizes that most people use, and because real long casts are not often required, nor are they usually a good fishing technique.

A more important disadvantage of spin-casting tackle is that it is hard to control the flight of the lure to achieve the pin-point accuracy that the spinning and bait caster can manage. The bait caster can slow the flight of the lure at any time with his thumb, and the spinning angler can do the same with his index finger, feathering the line as it comes off the exposed spool. But the spin caster has only two choices: stopping the lure abruptly by releasing the thumb stop, or casting with both hands, using one to control the rod and push the button, while the other is cupped around the reel, in position to finger the line as it comes through the hole in the reel housing. While both methods work, stopping the lure rapidly usually results in a splashy, inaccurate cast, and casting two-handed is not very natural or comfortable for a long day's fishing.

A final disadvantage of spin-casting tackle is that it is not suited to ultralight fishing. Tiny ultralight lures do not provide enough weight to pull the line through the restrictive hole in the reel, and light lines tend to foul inside the reel housing. In fact, six-pound line and three-eighths to five-eighths ounce lures represent the practical minimum that can be used satisfactorily with spin-casting tackle. You'll note in your shopping that a number of companies offer tiny spin-casting rods and reels that most people associate with ultralight fishing. These little outfits are lots of fun to fish with, and they cast and play fish well. But they will not satisfactorily handle light lines and lures, and light lines and tiny lures are what ultralight fishing is all about.

However, such minor limitations don't affect the majority of anglers. You should seriously consider spin-casting tackle if:

1. You want wide flexibility in lures and baits in the six- to fourteen-pound line range.
2. You care more about ruggedness and reliability in your equipment than sophistication and finesse.

3. You seldom need to cast with great distance or accuracy.

4. You often fish at night and want to use equipment that doesn't require good visibility to operate.

5. You don't plan to fish often in subfreezing temperatures (the wet line tends to freeze up inside the reel hood).

6. You're not interested in fishing with the lightest of lures and lines (or if you are interested, you have ultralight spinning gear to do it with).

The decision to go with spin-casting tackle simplifies some of your other decisions. Since ultralight enthusiasts usually choose spinning tackle, and those who need heavy equipment usually go for bait-casting, most spin-casting tackle falls in the "medium" class with rods running five to five and a half feet in length. Most reels come from the factory already spooled with monofilament, and the best makers fill their reels with the premium monofilament recommended earlier. When you select your spin-casting reel, you'll probably have a choice of line weights. Ten-pound test is probably most common, but eight-, fourteen-, and twenty-pound test are also available, with six-pound test offered on the "miniature" outfits described earlier.

A final advantage is that good quality spin-casting tackle is inexpensive. If you're looking for the least expensive way to find out if you like fishing, spin casting is the way to go. All of the major manufacturers offer complete systems of rod, reel, and line (sometimes with a couple of

FIGURE 5–3 Two high-quality spin-casting outfits. *Top:* Zebco 20/20 reel mounted on Pro Staff rod. *Bottom:* Johnson high-speed reel mounted on Heddon Magnagraph rod. (Photo by David Guiney)

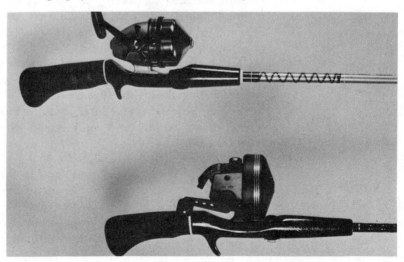

lures and a lure box thrown in) at a lower price than the components purchased separately. And discount stores carry more spin-casting tackle than any other kind and offer it at attractive prices.

Casting with Spin-Casting Tackle

Now for the casting. In the illustrations shown and in the instructions given, we're assuming that you want all the accuracy you can get out of your equipment. Therefore, the two-handed casting method is recommended. While most of your casts will be one-handed, you need to be proficient with the two-handed cast. With the illustrations, you'll be able to visualize how the one-handed cast would be performed.

TWO-HANDED CAST

Begin by holding the rod and reel as illustrated in Figure 5–4. The reel handles are up and the rod tip is aimed above the horizontal. Your left (line) hand is around the rod in front of the reel spool housing with your thumb and index finger holding the line lightly. Now depress the thumb button with your right hand, and feel the line slip out through your fingers as the lure or practice plug takes the line out. Practice letting the line slip through your fingers; once you get the feel of it, stop the plug at various points in the drop by tightening your fingers.

You can practice stopping the line completely with your fingers, slowing it down without stopping it, and stopping it after allowing the plug to fall a predetermined distance. But you're learning how that line hand can control line speed and lure accuracy.

When you're ready to cast, push the thumb button in all the way; this will stop the lure. Now all you have to do is release the button when you cast, and the plug is on its way. The rest of the process is exactly like casting with bait-casting tackle: assume a stance with your body angled a little toward the target; bring the rod up to ten o'clock and aim for the target; make the backcast, stopping the rod at one o'clock so that the lure can load it; without hesitation, make the forward power stroke; release the thumb button at about eleven o'clock; follow through. As with other types of casting, the distance between the rod tip and lure before the cast varies with the weight of the lure. Your lure trajectory depends on your release point: too high and you released too early; too low and you released too late.

Note carefully the use of the line hand in Figure 5–4. As the lure speeds toward the target, you can slow it down or stop it with your fingers. When you retrieve line, bring it in between those same fingers. Spin-casting reels spool the line most evenly when there's a little tension on it, and your fingers tend to keep the line clean, which helps to avoid some potential problems inside the reel housing.

FIGURE 5-4 Casting with spin-casting tackle (Illustration courtesy Zebco/Brunswick)

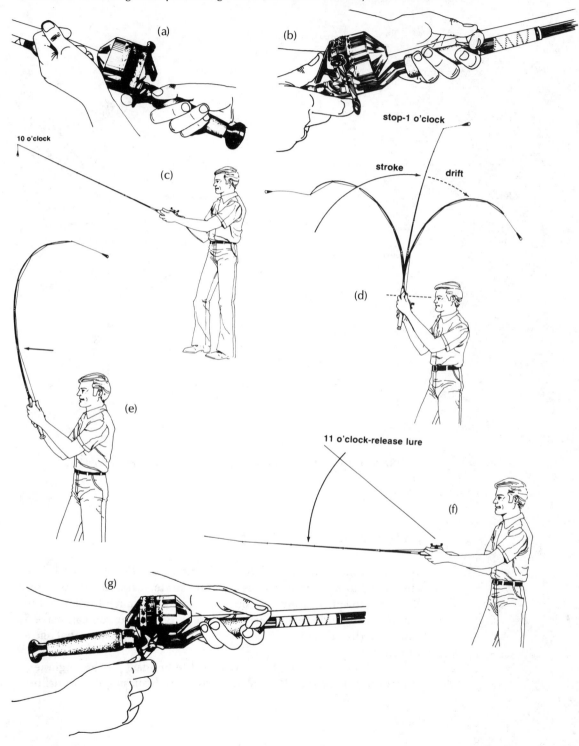

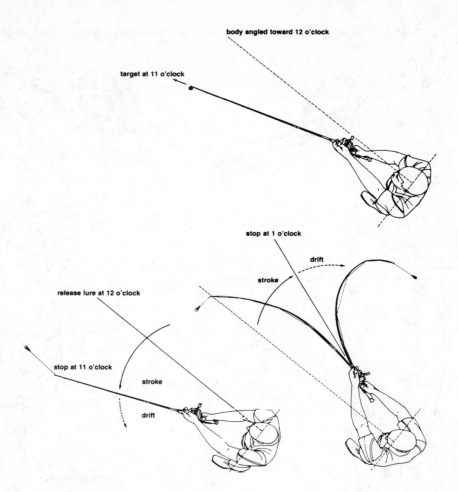

body angled toward 12 o'clock

target at 11 o'clock

stop at 1 o'clock

drift

stroke

release lure at 12 o'clock

stop at 11 o'clock

stroke

drift

FIGURE 5–5 The side cast (Illustration courtesy Zebco/Brunswick)

SIDE CAST AND UNDERHAND CASTING

As with the other casting tackle we've discussed, the side cast is one you'll need to master. Figure 5–5 will illustrate. Underhand casting is difficult with spin-casting gear because there's too much friction in the system for the little flip to carry the lure very far. But you can make a short underhand cast in a pinch, so you might want to practice that one a little, too.

     If a type of fishing gear can be said to be ideal for the beginner, spin-casting tackle is it. With it, you can learn the basics of most fishing techniques and handle all sorts of baits and lures from the top-water chuggers to the deep runners. If you later decide to move on to spinning or casting gear, you'll find the transition simple. And if you don't, you'll find your spin-casting tackle adequate for most of the fishing you want to do.

CHAPTER

6

Fishing with Bait

The early morning sun sparkled on the green river as we assembled our tackle. My friend Bob Cianelli and I had come to Virginia's Shenandoah River for smallmouth bass, and I was eager to cast my crayfish fly into the inviting current lines between the ledges and boulders.

"Let's seine a few hellgrammites before we start fishing," suggested Bob.

"But I'm fishing with flies, and I thought you were going to use spinners."

"The artificials will stop working when the sun gets high, and if we want to keep catching bass, we'll need the hellgrammites. Let's get 'em now before it gets too hot."

Now Bob Cianelli has fished the Shenandoah for years, and I'm not one to argue with the local experts. So we found a likely riffle, and I spread the net downstream while Bob turned over rocks, dislodging the nymphs and larvae clinging to the bottom. The rich Shenandoah soon yielded a couple of dozen hellgrammites, along with caddis larvae, stonefly nymphs, and one surprised crayfish. Bob dropped the wriggling hellgrammites in his belt bait box and released the other critters strug-

62

gling in the net. Then we rigged up as we had started to, me with the crayfish fly and Bob with the spinner.

We started catching bass immediately. Bob caught his share on the spinner, but my crayfish fly worked so well that Bob soon found himself interested in fly fishing. He learned rapidly and soon mastered the dead drift of the sunken fly, expertly hooking the bass as they picked up the fly even though a slight twitch of the floating line was the only indication of a take.

But as the morning drew on, the fishing slowed, and by noon we were no longer catching bass on spinners and flies, just as Bob had predicted. We ate lunch in the shade, and as we finished I looked at Bob.

"Time for the hellgrammites?"

"Yep."

We rigged light-action spinning rods with bait hooks, hooked the hellgrammites under the thorax "collar," and began tossing them softly quartering upstream into a riffle. The fish that had ignored our artificials for over an hour took the hellgrammites greedily, and we caught bass throughout the hot hours with the live bait. And the fish took the dead-drifted insect as softly as they took the sunken crayfish; now I knew how Bob had learned to fish the fly so rapidly. As the shadows lengthened again (and our hellgrammite supply was exhausted), we went back to spinner and fly and finished the day successfully.

You won't fish very long before you'll discover situations in which live bait will catch fish while artificials will not, just as we did that Shenandoah high noon. Skill in bait fishing can keep you from getting skunked when the fish insist on real food.

Properly speaking, bait fishing involves using organic material to attract the fish. Usually, live baits like hellgrammites, night crawlers, minnows, or insect larvae are used. Sometimes, prepared baits are utilized; for example, preserved minnows, salmon eggs, or even canned corn!

ADVANTAGES

Fishing with bait has a number of advantages. Most importantly, the bait angler can appeal to the fish's sense of taste and smell as well as vision. These chemical senses are highly developed in fish, and artificial lures cannot appeal to them. This is one reason why bait fishing is often effective during high and cloudy water conditions when other methods are not very productive.

Another advantage is that live bait provides a natural and appealing action that artificial lures usually cannot equal. Also, natural baits don't just represent the foods that fish are used to eating—they *are* the foods the fish are used to eating!

Finally, fish tend to take live bait deeply and to hold on to it longer, making the fish easier to hook and less likely to escape during the playing and landing process. With artificial lures, on the other hand, if the fish is not hooked the instant it strikes the artificial, it will expel the lure. Beginners usually find it easier to hook and land fish using live bait.

DISADVANTAGES

Of course, there are some disadvantages in bait fishing. For one thing, time or money must be devoted to collecting live bait. This is not to say that collecting bait is unpleasant; indeed, for many fishermen it is an essential part of the total fishing experience. Still, the time spent collecting bait is time that is not spent fishing. If the angler chooses to purchase bait rather than investing the time to collect it, he makes an expenditure on a highly perishable item. A purchase of an artificial lure can be spread over many fishing trips, but bait is used only once and must be replaced on the next outing.

Live bait also poses problems of transport and storage. Plan to spend some time and money on the problem of keeping live bait alive and fresh, as well as on collecting it.

Finally, the tendency of fish to take bait deeply can sometimes be a disadvantage. Many deeply-hooked fish are fatally injured and will not survive even if promptly released. Most anglers regret killing an undersized game fish, but the little fellows are just as vulnerable to live bait as the big ones. Gut-hooked fish usually don't survive, whatever their size. More and more streams are being restricted to artificial lures only, so that the sport fishery can be utilized to the maximum enjoyment of many anglers. The live bait artist will have to develop skill with artificials if he wishes to fish these restricted waters.

Live Bait

In the beginning was the worm . . .

For centuries anglers have gathered and stored worms for fishing. Many still do, but today worms are being raised commercially on a giant scale and not just for fishing. Because worms rapidly turn organic waste into protein, some communities are now using worms to process municipal wastes. Worms are being studied by scientists as a possible human food. The first "wormburger" is already a reality, at least at the experimental level.

Most "worm farming" is still devoted to producing worms for fishing, and it is big business, indeed. Today worms are sold not only over the counter, but also prepackaged in vending machines!

Fishing with worms is probably the best way to get started in bait fishing. The equipment needed is not expensive, the bait is readily available, and worms will attract most fish you might be interested in fishing for.

BOBBER METHOD

The simplest method for beginners is to use a bobber, suspending the baited hook at a selected distance beneath the surface. By adjusting the position of the bobber (see the preceding chapter), various depths can be fished until the most productive one is located. The bobber gives a visual indication of a bite, and the hook is set when the bobber is pulled under the surface by the strike.

The bobber method can be employed in stationary fishing from the bank or an anchored boat or in drift fishing. In the drift method, the boat or canoe is allowed to drift with the current or the breeze while the worm and bobber drift alongside. The worm can be made to cover a lot of territory using the drift method.

A stationary angler can also cover the water using a bobber and worm rig, especially if he is fishing a moving stream. By casting the worm and bobber upstream, you can drift them through productive water until the worm reaches a point downstream from your position where it can be allowed to remain stationary for a time, drifted on downstream by paying out additional slack line, or retrieved for another upstream cast.

Many beginners use bobbers that are too large. Remember that the bobber provides some resistance to the fish when it takes the worm, and that resistance may alarm the fish before it takes the worm deeply enough to be hooked. The smallest bobber that you can see easily should be used.

BOTTOM-FISHING TECHNIQUE

Another method of fishing with worms is the bottom-fishing technique. Here a sinker is the terminal gear; the hook is attached at some point above the sinker, often with a "standoff" or a three-way swivel that holds the hook at a right angle to the line. In flowing water, the bait may be kept in one location by using a heavy sinker or allowed to bounce along close to the bottom if a lighter sinker is used.

Like the bobber, a sinker provides some resistance that may alert the fish, so the smallest that will do the job is best. Experienced anglers usually prefer the bottom-fishing method. With this technique, you don't have to guess how far the worm is off the bottom as you do with the bobber setup, and the bottom method presents the worm in a somewhat more natural manner than the bobber technique does. You'll find it

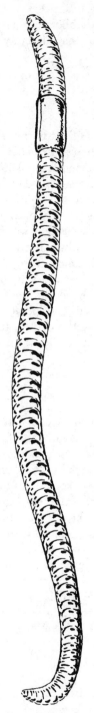

FIGURE 6–1
Nightcrawler

more difficult to detect subtle strikes than with the bobber, but since there will probably be more action near the bottom, that difficulty is offset, even for the beginner.

UPSTREAM METHOD

Undoubtedly the most sophisticated worm-fishing method is the upstream method. With the leader weighted just enough to sink the bait to the desired level, the worm is cast upstream from the angler's position and allowed to drift back toward him. This procedure presents the worm under the most natural condition—drifting almost as freely as if unattached. The difficulty in the technique is in detecting the strike. Since there must be at least a tiny amount of slack in the line to allow for the free drift of the worm, the strike of the fish is extremely subtle, requiring an experienced hand and eye for detecting the strike and setting the hook. In actuality, the technique is exactly like fishing the artificial nymph upstream, and that's regarded by fly anglers as the most demanding of the fly-fishing skills. If you decide to try this technique, begin by using one of the smaller bobbers to help in following the drift of the worm; then discard the visual aid once you get the feel of it.

HOOKING THE WORM

This method of hooking the worm may influence your success, too. Worms are most attractive to fish when they can wiggle; therefore hooking them lightly through the body provides the best action. Attached in this way, the worm is easily pulled off the hook by a fish, and you'll probably lose a lot of worms to small sunfish if you hook them this way. If you hook the worm through the "collar" (the enlarged, light-colored section about a third of the way back from the head), the worm will be more difficult for a mouthing fish to pull off the hook. But since the collar area is the location of some vital organs, the worm will not last as long when hooked in this way. If you're fishing where some sizable gamefish are to be found, hook your worms loosely and hang the losses; you'll attract more of the bigger fish that way. But if you're fishing where most of the takers will be small sunfish, thread the worm on the hook and leave only a small portion to wiggle. Otherwise, the little fellows will pick your pocket time after time.

Fishing with Bait Fish

Although it has been nearly thirty years ago, I remember as if it were yesterday. On Friday afternoons, Dad and I would take the minnow net and head for our secret creek. We would spread the net on the surface,

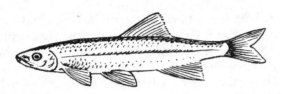

FIGURE 6–2
A typical bait fish

let it sink to the bottom, and toss in pieces of bread to draw the minnows. After a few minutes, we lifted the net swiftly, spread it on the soft grass beside the stream, and selected the number and size of minnows we wanted for the next day's crappie fishing trip.

I visited the secret creek a couple of years ago. It's silted in now, a victim of careless housing development on the surrounding land, and no minnows are there. But where minnows can still be found, they are superior bait, not only for crappie, but for many other game fish and pan fish as well.

Most species of small fish are good for bait. But be sure not to use small game fish by mistake—such use is illegal in most states. And remember that bait fish taken from cold water streams will not live long in warm water, such as is found in rivers and farm ponds.

Before selecting the bait fish you want to use, be sure to find out what restrictions, if any, apply in your area. Many a small stream and farm pond has been taken over by "trash" fish first introduced as bait, and some states have specific limitations on what species may be used and where. And if you fish with live minnows, do not release the survivors at the end of your fishing day unless you caught them in the same body of water. Be particularly careful of small lakes and ponds, because they are quite vulnerable to species introduced from the outside environment.

Like worms, minnows are often fished with bobbers. But in fishing with minnows, the bobber not only signals the strike, but may be used to restrain the minnow from swimming into underwater debris and taking the hook with it.

The minnow can be hooked through the lips, through the tail, or through the back, either just behind or in front of the dorsal fin. What you want is a minnow that can swim vigorously and with endurance, but at the same time communicate injury to a predatory game fish. Experiment until you find the hooking procedure that works best.

A few anglers use a "minnow harness," a setup that lashes the minnow into position over the hook without actually impaling it. Minnow harnesses are hard to find now in many parts of the country, but if durability is a problem in your minnows, you might find the harness beneficial. If you intend to cast a minnow repeatedly, as you would a lure, a minnow harness is essential.

67   Sometimes it is desirable to allow the bait fish to swim freely without the bobber to restrain it. If you know the area you will fish is mostly free from snags or if the direction and depth of the minnow can be controlled by line manipulation, this method can be used. It is especially effective when used with large minnows. Large bait fish will usually attract the larger predator fish. If you choose to fish with big shiners or chubs or suckers, you may attract only a few takers, but those are likely to be braggin'-sized fish.

Fishing with bait fish can be nerve-wracking at times, especially for the neophyte. Predator fish usually attack a minnow from the side, sometimes repeatedly, before finally killing it. And since some bait fish have spiney dorsal fins, the attacker may swallow the fish only head first, so the dorsal fin won't stick in its throat on the way down. What all this means is that you might have to wait several minutes for a fish to take a minnow deeply enough to be hooked.

Bait fish must be kept fresh and vigorous to be effective in fishing for most species. Catfish are an exception; they often like dead minnows as well as live ones.

Other Natural Baits

INSECT LARVAE

The immature stages of aquatic insects make up a large portion of the diet of most fish. These forms, called larvae by entomologists and nymphs by fishermen, can be found clinging to the bottom rubble of streams, under rocks, or burrowed in the silt of the bottom. The fly angler imitates the insects with specialized flies, but it is possible to fish the real larvae as live bait.

The major problem in fishing live insect larvae is that most of them are quite fragile. For this reason, it is not feasible to fish them in situations where repeated casting is required; they won't stay on the hook under such conditions. Live larvae are best used when they can be softly swung or lobbed into prime locations or where the current can be used to carry the bait to the suspected location of the fish. A fly rod or soft-action spinning outfit is best for fishing like this.

Here's a specific rundown on a few of the major larvae.

Mayfly Nymphs. Mayfly nymphs are the immature stages of the upright-winged insects that are found in many trout streams and some warm-water streams. The adult forms are so delicate that fishing them live is impossible; in fact, that is the reason that fly fishing was invented a couple of thousand years ago. The larger nymphs, however, can be fished if you take special pains.

Mayfly nymphs can be collected from the bottoms of rocks on the stream bed. They are usually small, requiring hook sizes from ten to

FIGURE 6–3
Mayfly nymph (*top*) and
stonefly nymph

FIGURE 6–4
Caddis larva

FIGURE 6–5 Hellgrammite

sixteen or eighteen, and they range in color from brown to gray to black. If the stream has vegetation growing along the shoreline or in slowly flowing sections of the main current, mayfly nymphs can be found in the roots of the vegetation or clinging to the underwater parts of the plants. Fishermen who work together in collecting bait can usually get the burrowing types of mayflies if one of them holds a net against the bottom while another stirs up the stream bed upstream.

Mayfly nymphs can be fished only by using the lightest of hooks. Many live-bait artists use the light-wire hooks designed for tying dry flies, because the heavier wire of standard hooks will break the nymph apart upon being pushed through them. Don't plan on casting mayfly nymphs at all. The nymph should be gently lowered into the water and allowed to wash downstream into the suspected lie of the fish. All in all, fishing with live mayfly nymphs is possible but not very practical.

Stonefly Nymphs. As a group, the stonefly nymphs are larger than the mayfly species, requiring hooks sized six to ten in most instances. These nymphs are found in greatest numbers in riffles where they cling to the undersides of rocks. Stonefly nymphs have two tails (most mayfly nymphs have three), and they always have prominent antennae. If not brown or black, they usually show strongly contrasting colors, yellow and brown being most common.

Stonefly nymphs are a little more durable than mayfly nymphs, but casting is still out of the question in most instances. Because stonefly nymphs cannot swim, you should allow them to drift without added motion.

Caddis Nymphs. Caddis larvae are sometimes called "rock worms," because their worm-like bodies are found stuck to the bottoms of stream rocks. Most caddis larvae are protected by cases which the insects build from stream materials stuck together by a mucus secreted by the larvae. Each genus of caddis flies (and there are many) builds a distinctive case. Most common are the rounded cases made of tiny pebbles and sand grains. Fish will eat case and all; therefore you can remove the whole business from the stream bottom and thread it on the hook. Because the case adds durability, caddis nymphs fished in this way can be cast softly a few times, but they are still subject to rapid deterioration if treated roughly. If you prefer to fish the uncased larvae, they can be removed from the case and threaded onto a light wire hook.

Hellgrammites. Of all the immature insects available in most waters, the hellgrammites are the most important to the bait fisherman. This ugly insect is the larva of the dobson fly, and it is a real mouthful, up to two or three inches long. Smallmouth bass have a special fondness for hellgrammites, but all game fish will take them in waters where they are common.

Hellgrammites are much more durable than other nymphs. They are not only much larger, but have a leathery skeleton that is able to stand up to careful casting. They are best hooked through the collar (thorax) just behind the head. Thread the entire hook bend under the collar; then turn the bend and barb so that it emerges above the thorax. This does not injure the insect too badly, but provides a secure hold and allows it to curl into a tight ball, which is the form in which the fish most often see hellgrammites. Be careful of the strong mandibles at the head; they can deliver a painful pinch, strong enough to draw blood. Many anglers like to clip off the pinchers found at the anterior end of the hellgrammite, because they are used to grab the bottom and pull the insect under rocks and other obstructions. By clipping these, you assure that the hellgrammite will be unable to take your line back under a snag.

Like other insect larvae, hellgrammites are found on the bottoms of rocks, especially in swift and well-aerated water. Because they tend to wash off rocks as they are lifted from the bottom, hellgrammites are easy to collect in a net or seine. Two fishermen working together can best collect hellgrammites. One holds a net or wire screen downstream while the other turns rocks over, washing the insects into the seine.

Mature Insects. Most mature insects are too small or fragile to be used in live bait fishing. Among the important exceptions are grasshoppers and crickets. These can be gathered and fished with bobbers. Most "hoppers" and crickets, however, are taken by fish from the surface of the water after being blown in or hopping the wrong way. It is difficult for the bait fisherman to present the insects in this way, since they won't take casting.

FIGURE 6–6 Grasshopper

Some hopper and cricket fishermen prowl the banks of meadow streams, well back from the water, looking for signs of feeding fish. Upon sighting a potential customer, they crawl closer and gently lower a hopper or cricket onto the surface. This technique is called "dapping," and it can be used with artificial flies, as well as live insects.

Hoppers and crickets are inactive in the early morning hours, but become active once the sun warms their bodies. Collect them early when they are easy to catch. Fish them later when the insects are active and likely to be on the water.

Another insect that can be seasonally important is the inch worm. These small green worms lower themselves from trees above the stream on thin strands of silk. When they touch the surface, they are pulled slightly downstream against the fine strand, making a small "V" wake on the surface. When fish are feeding on these creatures, drifting an inch worm downstream with an occasional pause to create the wake can be a deadly tactic.

FIGURE 6–7 Cricket

CRAYFISH

The crayfish ("crawdad" to Southerners) is a favorite of game fish wherever it is found. Some studies have shown that smallmouth bass prefer crayfish to all other food and choose them for up to ninety percent of their diet when large populations are available. Like other crustaceans, crayfish must periodically shed their shells (exoskeletons) as they grow, and they are especially delectable to fish when in this "peeler" stage.

You may collect a few crayfish accidentally while seining hellgrammites, since they favor the same kind of water. Some small creeks have so many crayfish that they are relatively easy to gather. Typically, weed-infested streams have large populations, because the alkaline waters that promote weed growth are also congenial to the crayfish, because they need calcium and other minerals for shell formation.

Live crayfish are best fished in the early morning or late evening hours or at night when they are naturally most active. They produce the most appealing action when hooked through one of the shell segments near the tail. Hook them, like the hellgrammite, by sliding the entire hook bend under a shell segment; then turn the bend and barb so that it slides over the outside of the shell. When the bottom conditions allow it, fish the crayfish on a slack line so that it can clamber around naturally. Leave the bail open on a spinning reel or strip off some slack if you use casting equipment, and hold the loose line in your fingers so that you can detect a fish picking up the crayfish. In waters with little current, a fish will usually pick up a crayfish and carry it for some distance before swallowing it. A good strategy in such conditions is to allow the fish to carry the bait away until it stops, wait for a pause while the fish begins to swallow the crayfish, and then set the hook when the fish moves away with it again. In fast-flowing streams, the fish will take the crayfish more quickly, but you must still allow enough time for the bait to be swallowed before setting the hook.

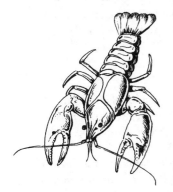

FIGURE 6-8 Crayfish

FROGS

While they are excellent bait, especially for bass, frogs are difficult to fish properly. Many anglers who fish with frogs cast them from boat to shoreline and then retrieve them back toward the boat again. In fact, however, free frogs never swim toward open water, so this is not a natural presentation, though it may take fish. Frogs spend most of their time near shore, in weed beds, or resting on lily pads or other large vegetation, and they leave these areas only to move through small patches of water toward another resting place. Most of this movement is either parallel to the shore line or toward the bank, not away from it, and this movement is difficult for the angler to represent from a boat some distance away. A better presentation is to offer the frog from the shoreline where the natural movements can be more closely approximated. Here, however, the problem is spooking the fish before you can get the frog to them.

Most anglers who fish with frogs either hook them through the lips or use a "frog harness." You can find the equipment you need to fish frogs in catalogs, but you probably won't find the frogs themselves in bait stores. You'll have to catch them yourself.

Gathering, Storing, and Preserving Live Bait

Efficient collection, storage, and transport of live bait is essential if you are to succeed as a bait fisherman. Here are a few tips.

WORMS

Fishing worms, of course, can be dug. This involves a lot of effort and no assurance of success and usually produces rather small garden worms. A more efficient method is to collect nightcrawlers right off the top of the ground.

Nightcrawlers come to the surface on warm nights after a shower or a heavy dew. Your lawn is a good place to look for them, or you can check the local golf course. You need a light to locate the worms, but they are sensitive to light and will retreat into their burrows if you shine it directly on them. If you use a flashlight, try to shine it at an angle to the ground. Even better, tape some red cellophane over the lens before beginning the collecting process.

When you find a worm, be prepared for the fact that a portion of it is probably in the burrow already. When you grasp the exposed portion, the worm will pull strongly down in an attempt to escape into the burrow. Don't pull back. The worm will break in two if you do. Instead, just hold on firmly to your portion until the worm tires of pulling against you. Then pull the worm out of the burrow and add it to your collection.

You can store your worms in dirt or in the commercial worm "bedding" that is sold in tackle shops. A good home mixture is a little loose dirt with a lot of damp leaf fragments; the leaves provide organic material that the worms can eat. Be sure to check your worm box periodically, and remove any dead worms promptly. Most fatalities occur right after the original collection, since a few worms are usually injured in the tug-of-war with the angler. Be sure to keep your worms in a cool place.

Worms are easy to carry on fishing trips. A little dirt and shade to keep them cool are sufficient. Belt-loop boxes are available for the wading fisherman, but almost any container that can be kept cool and moist is okay for the boating angler.

BAIT FISH

Preserving minnows or other bait fish is more of a challenge than worm storage. The little fish die as soon as they exhaust the oxygen of the water they are kept in; thus, long-term storage requires electric aerators to replenish the oxygen supply. Some of these aerators have receptacles that can be plugged into auto cigarette lighters for use in transit; others can run off the batteries that propel electric trolling motors. If you keep bait fish at home for long periods, a regular home aquarium with aerator may suffice, as long as you use water that does not have chlorine in it. If you want to keep a big supply on hand, an old bathtub with a commercial-duty aerator is the answer.

If you live near a stream where your bait fish may be kept without fear of theft, a homemade or commercial bait cage can keep them in good condition for a long time if food is provided regularly.

On the fishing trip itself, many anglers make use of the minnow bucket, which can be lowered into the river or lake once the fishing location is reached. Still, the bucket may not be suitable for transporting the bait unless the trip is a short one. Remember that active, vigorous bait fish are essential to success, and the oxygen supply is most important in keeping your minnows in good condition. Oxygen tablets may be sufficient for short periods.

INSECT LARVAE

Most anglers don't bother trying to store the small larvae of the mayflies and stoneflies; they are easier to gather on the stream than to store and transport. Hellgrammites are sometimes an exception. Since they are becoming harder to find on many streams, you may want to store leftovers for another day or build up a good supply when a favorable habitat is located.

The ideal storage medium for hellgrammites is probably the commercial bedding, but a good alternative is ordinary sawdust, kept moist but not soaked. The larvae will burrow into the sawdust and can last a month or so if the box is kept in a cool, dark location and the proper moisture is maintained. It is important not to overcrowd your hellgrammites. They are vicious and will attack one another if you put too many together in a small area.

CRAYFISH

Crayfish are difficult to catch without the use of a crayfish trap unless you find an unusually fertile creek. The traps can be ordered from catalogs or purchased in tackle shops. Leave them in a likely location overnight with a couple of dead fish in the bottom.

If you lack a trap and want to catch just a few crawdads for a fishing trip, try turning over rocks in a riffly area. You might find it easier to catch the scuttling crayfish if you take a tomato juice can and cut both ends out; drop the can over the crayfish and reach in and remove it with your other hand.

Don't plan on keeping crayfish for any length of time unless you have a cool stream available to you. A spring house is ideal if you can get the use of one. For storage during fishing trips, damp moss is satisfactory.

Preserved and Prepared Baits

In addition to the live baits, many prepared baits are available, both in commercial and homemade form. Here's a sample.

PICKLED MINNOWS

These are minnows packed in a preservative and sold in a jar. While not usually as effective as live minnows, they can be useful under certain conditions, and they are certainly handy when live minnows are difficult or impossible to gather.

Preserved minnows can be used effectively in bottom fishing for catfish, although freshly killed minnows are preferable when available. Pickled minnows are also good shortly after the spring thaw when game fish are slowly becoming more active as their metabolism speeds up with the warming of the water.

A lot of anglers use preserved minnows almost like a lure, by using a special technique to present the minnow. A large sewing needle is employed, one in which the eye has been filed open on one side so that inserting the monofilament fishing line is easy. A "mono" loop is inserted into the eye of the needle, and then the needle threaded through the minnow, starting through the mouth and being drawn out just behind the anal fin, pulling the line behind it. The loop is then removed from the needle and secured to a treble hook, which is drawn up tight beneath the minnow's belly. If you hook your minnow this way, it can be cast, manipulated, and retrieved just like a lure. Such a rig can be especially effective in fast water where the fish must make a quick decision to strike without giving the minnow careful scrutiny.

SALMON EGGS

Salmon eggs are a favorite bait of the trout fisherman, most especially in early-season fishing for hatchery trout. Salmon eggs are sold like pickled minnows, packed in jars in pickling fluid. Belt attachments make it possible to get at the eggs without unscrewing the lid repeatedly. Salmon eggs are generally pink or yellow, but they are sold in "hot" and fluorescent colors, too, which make them more visible during cloudy water conditions.

The main trick with salmon eggs is hooking them so that they don't come off the hook at the first nibble. The "bait-holder" hooks sold by Eagle Claw are a big help in this regard, but the method of hooking the eggs is important, too. The best method is to run the point of the hook, not into the middle of the egg, but just under the skin so that the bend and barb of the hook are covered while the soft center of the egg rests in the protective bend of the hook. Even with this method, salmon eggs are tough to keep on the hook; you'll find that the toughness of the eggs varies from jar to jar, and most of them will not stay hooked if you do much casting.

When salmon eggs are used for steelhead trout, Pacific salmon, and other large species, they are often fished in a mesh bag with the hook hidden inside. This arrangement is more durable than the single egg method, but it is not applicable to most ordinary trout fishing.

Although salmon eggs are most effective on hatchery trout, they are also a killing bait on streams where salmon actually spawn, including many in Alaska, Canada, and the Pacific Northwest. During salmon spawning, trout and other fish lie downstream of the spawning beds and feast on the rich eggs that wash down to them. In some cases they will actually invade the nesting sites. Even purist fly anglers have invented salmon egg "flies" to fish under such conditions.

CHEESE AND CORN

You might not be aware that the neighborhood supermarket can be a source of effective fishing bait. Both cheese and canned corn are favorites of fishermen seeking hatchery trout.

FIGURE 6–9 Opening day of trout season. You can bet that most of these anglers are using cheese, corn, or salmon eggs. (Photo courtesy U.S. Fish and Wildlife Service. Photo by John Boaze)

Yellow corn, preferably of the large-kernel variety, is fixed on the hook much like a salmon egg. The point is inserted just under the skin and the kernel manipulated on the hook so that the tender center portion is protected by the hook bend.

Most cheese users prefer the pasteurized process type cheese, such as Velveeta. This type of cheese is heavily laced with milk solids; so it is gummy and will stay on the hook better than crumbly cheddar-type cheeses. Mold it into a ball and press it onto the hook, obscuring the point and barb.

Cheese, corn, and salmon eggs are usually fished deep with added weight in the form of sinkers or split shot to get them down. Although it is possible to fish these baits suspended from bobbers in quiet streams, most skilled anglers prefer to fish them just off the bottom, keeping slack line controlled so that strikes can be detected. Fly rods and soft-action spinning outfits are good for such fishing, because these delicate baits have to be cast very softly to keep them on the hook.

DOUGH BALLS

Dough balls are prepared baits used mostly for carp and catfish fishing. A lot of commercial preparations are available, and many anglers have a favorite "home-brew" recipe for dough balls. Dough balls are fished deep, because the carp and catfish that they attract are bottom feeders.

SUMMARY

By now it should be clear that bait fishing is much more complex and sophisticated than many people believe. The skilled bait fisherman is a skilled angler, indeed. Not only is the method productive in itself, but the techniques, with slight modification, are useful in fishing with artificial lures and flies. Bait fishing, then, is often the foundation of the expert angler's bag of tricks.

It can be argued that fishing with artificial lures is more sporting than bait fishing. But fishing with artificials is not more effective under most conditions. For the angler who wants to eat the catch, for the beginner who wants some results without too much hassle, for the veteran who likes to keep it simple, fishing with bait is hard to beat.

CHAPTER 7

Fishing with Artificial Lures

Of all the aspects of fishing, none is more confusing to the beginner than fishing with artificial lures. Even veteran anglers are dazzled by the array of lures available today, each of them advertised as if its possession is absolutely essential to fishing success. And yet, with only a few exceptions, the ads that work so hard to sell you a given lure don't tell you how to use it or where or for what fish or under what conditions. Instead, they usually picture an angler groaning under the weight of a full stringer of monster fish, creating the impression that all you have to do is buy the lure and drop it in the water, and you'll catch so many fish that you'll need help hauling them home.

It's not that simple. To use artificial lures successfully, you need to know about how they work and how fish respond to them, and you need to cast them on properly selected line with a compatible rod and reel. You need to select the lure in light of the conditions you face. Are the fish deep over bottom cover or working the surface for bait fish? Are they cruising from place to place feeding on whatever they find, or are they

holding in one particular depth or location feeding on the same food repeatedly? Are they chasing their food or letting it come to them? Is the water clear or cloudy or downright muddy? The list of questions goes on and on. Sometimes you choose a lure because you know the answer. More often, you choose one hoping it will help you find the answer. Either way, you need to know lures to make a good selection.

It's not possible here to deal with all the lures you'll have to choose from, but some of the confusion can be eliminated by grouping artificials according to *type*. Look at it this way: It's possible to make generalizations about types of lures, information that you can then apply with some confidence to specific lures within that category. We'll consider spinners, plugs, jigs, spoons, and plastic lures. Flies are a whole story in themselves, and we'll save that category for another chapter.

Spinners

Spinners get their name from their most prominent feature: a metal blade (or blades) that revolves around a stationary shaft as the lure is pulled through the water. Spinners came into popularity with spinning tackle, and they are still best suited to that type of tackle, especially in the lighter sizes. Spin-casting tackle and modern lightweight bait-casting gear can handle spinners in the medium-weight range and up.

It seems likely that the flashing light patterns created by the spinning blades may simulate the scales of moving bait fish. It may also be that the vibrations and general underwater disturbance set up by the blades is the attractive element. Whatever the attraction, spinners are responsible for taking record fish year in and year out. In part, that's because anglers have confidence in spinners and fish them frequently, but that, in turn, is due to the popularity of spinners with the fish.

WEIGHT

Most spinners combine blades of silver, brass, or enamel with colored beads and hooks dressed with feathers of animal hair. Freshwater spinning commonly calls for spinners in a weight range from one-sixteenth ounce to one ounce. Occasionally spinners up to two ounces are used in freshwater angling, but these heavyweights are more common in saltwater fishing.

Spinning lures in the one-sixteenth- to one-quarter-ounce range are considered *ultralight,* and those from five-sixteenth- to three-eighths ounce *light.* The ultralight lures can be cast only with spinning tackle; they don't have enough weight to get a casting reel revolving or to overcome the friction imposed by the housing on a spin-cast reel. Ultralight spinners are usually fished on four-pound test line, occasionally on two-pound test. Lures in the light category call for four- to six-pound line. Most good quality spin-cast reels can handle six-pound line and light spinners, and the best of the bait-casting gear can, too, if carefully maintained and expertly used. Most beginners, though, will do better to stick with spinning gear for light lures. Remember that by carrying extra reel spools you can fish four-, six-, and eight-pound line with the same outfit; you don't have such versatility with spin-casting or bait-casting tackle.

Lures in the three-eighth- to one-half-ounce range would be considered *medium* weight, suited to line of six- to eight-pound test. In this weight range, spin- and bait-casting tackle is well suited as far as casting ease is concerned. One-half ounce and up moves into what most anglers would consider *heavy* spinning, at least in freshwater. In this range, too, you can pick your tackle.

BLADE SHAPE

Weight is not the only variable to take into consideration when selecting a spinner for a given application. *Blade shape* is more important than many anglers realize. The more rounded the spinner blade, the more resistance it provides in the water; therefore, a rounded blade will spin readily in slow water and at slow speeds of retrieve. A round blade also stands out from the shaft at a greater angle than faster spinning blades. Thus, you might choose a rounded-blade spinner for upstream casting and slow retrieves or for pond or lake fishing where there is no current to help the blade spin. This type of spinner is also a good choice for "buzzing" right across the surface, because the resistance of the round blade causes the spinner to run shallower and shallower as the retrieve speed is increased.

Because more oval-shaped blades cause the spinner to run deeper, they are good choices when you fish waters of moderate depth. Since these blades spin somewhat closer to the spinner shaft than the round ones, they do not spin as easily and are not suited to slow retrieves unless they are being drawn upstream against the current.

The long, pointed, "willow leaf" type spinner blade is best suited to deep and swift currents that would cause the more rounded blades to rise up away from the fish's location. To summarize, then, use the rounded blade when you want to fish shallow and slowly, the long, pointed blade when you want to fish deep and fast, and the oval blade for in-between situations.

BLADE COLOR

Another consideration is blade color. In very clear water, bright blades sometimes alarm fish, especially in the larger spinners. For such conditions, enameled blades with less flash may be more productive.

RETRIEVE

One of the best things about spinners from the standpoint of the beginner is that you can hardly fish them improperly. As long as you keep the blade spinning most of the time, you'll catch something with a spinner sooner or later. On the other hand, you can probably improve your success if you're a little bit imaginative. A lot of anglers just toss a spinner out and wind it back in without much thought to the whole process. But you can experiment, for example, by varying speeds on your retrieve.

Remember that with a spinner, the speed of the retrieve affects not only the overall speed of the lure, but also the rate of blade rotation and the vibrations and light flashes associated with it. Sometimes the fish want the thing buzzed in as fast as you can crank the reel handle; at other times, especially when the water is low and clear, they'll respond to a retrieve so slow that the blade barely turns.

An irregular rhythm to the retrieve is good, too. With most spinners, when you stop cranking the reel handle, the blade stops spinning and the lure nosedives; when you start winding again, the lure levels out and the blade resumes turning. I've found that a routine of three handle revolutions—pause—three more—pause is often effective when a steady retrieve won't do the trick. You can also experiment with what I call "drawing" the spinner. Instead of winding the spinner in, you pull it toward you with the rod tip; then wind up the slack line as you drop the tip for another "draw." This procedure has all the elements of the pause retrieve, but adds another enticement—continuously varying blade speed. At the beginning of the rod lift, the blade speed is slow; it speeds up as the lure is drawn toward you and tapers off again as you drop the rod tip to take up the slack line. One important tip: Be careful not to draw the lure too far at a time. You'll create so much slack that the line won't spool properly, or you won't be able to set the hook should a fish pick up the spinner as it falls during the pause in your retrieve.

In short, experiment. A good spinner will catch fish if you tie it to your toe and swim across a river, but it'll catch a lot more if you add your imagination to the action the designer has supplied.

SPINNERBAIT

A recent addition to the family of spinner-type lures is the *spinnerbait*, which consists of a spinner and a jig with a wire apparatus in between to which the line is attached, as shown in Figure 7–7. Because each part of the lure is attached to its own shaft, the spinner and jig work independently. Usually the hook is attached to the jig portion of the lure and is obscured by a rubber skirt or soft plastic lure body. Although spinner baits are fished at all levels, "buzzing" them across the surface is a favorite tactic, especially when the fish are sulking and seem uninterested in more subtle presentations. Because of the weight and blade resistance of these baits, they may require specially geared reels for repeated high speed retrieves.

Although treble-hook spinners are the rule, a number of manufacturers offer single-hook spinners. Many anglers believe that single-hook spinners hook fish more reliably than the treble-hook models, and they are also less likely to catch in snags so they are often chosen for use in brushy and obstructed waters. Single hooks are also lighter in weight than comparable treble hooks, an important consideration in the ultralight sizes. And, a single hook on a light spinner can be of larger bite and gap than a treble hook of the same weight. Finally, catch-and-release anglers have found that single hooks, especially barbless ones, harm fish less often and are far easier to remove than treble hooks. For these reasons, many of the "special regulation" areas that allow spinning specify that single-hook lures must be used. If the single-hook spinners you want are not available, you can modify the standard ones yourself by replacing the trebles with ring-eye, straight shank hooks of a similar size or even a size or two larger.

Finally, be sure to consider the benefits of adding the flash and

FIGURE 7–1 A selection of popular spinning lures. *Top:* Panther-Martin models. *Bottom:* Mepps spinners. (Photo by David Guiney)

appeal of the spinner to your bait fishing. You will find that many snelled bait hooks have a spinner blade or two. Even if you're a stationary bait angler, the spinner blades might attract a strike when you reel in to check or change baits. And if you fish live bait with movement, a spinner is likely to add to its appeal.

There are many makers of spinners. Mepps and Panther Martin are two of the most prominent, and a selection of their offerings is shown in Figure 7–1. You can be sure that you will catch fish using spinners. Just about every angler does, and most of them will be glad to share their favorite designs with you.

Plugs

Plugs are made from balsa wood, cork, and, in nearly all cases today, plastic. They look a little like bait fish in most cases, but they also represent frogs, snakes, crayfish, mice, birds, and nothing in particular.

Although the situation has changed somewhat since spin-casting tackle has become popular, for a long time plugs were so typically cast with bait-casting gear that this type of tackle is also known as "plug-casting" equipment. Today's angler can choose spinning tackle, especially for the lighter plugs, but most plugs today are probably hurled from spin-casting tackle. The real experts, though, still consider the bait-casting rig unsurpassed for plugging. And in the hands of those experts, it is.

To simplify the discussion a bit, we can group plugs into three categories: surface, floating-diving, and underwater (full-sinking) types.

FIGURE 7–2 Three types of plugs

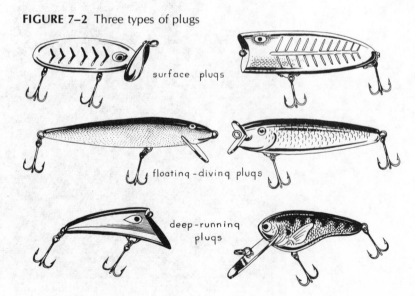

surface plugs

floating-diving plugs

deep-running plugs

SURFACE PLUGS

Surface plugs are made of hollow plastic or wood; they float all the time. The variety called a *popping plug* has a concave face that pushes a bubble of water before it on the retrieve, and if the plug is jerked or twitched suddenly, it makes a popping sound. A typical fishing technique is to allow the plug to lie quietly after first landing on the surface and then to begin the retrieve after the initial disturbance has died down. Poppers are most often fished along weed beds and shorelines in the early morning or late evening. Like other surface lures, they are also effective when pitched into a swirling school of fish feeding on the surface. The "Hula Popper" from the Fred Arbogast Company is typical of the breed and probably the all-time favorite of the popping plugs.

A similar group of plugs is called *disturbers*. These plugs have various attachments that disturb the surface when they are manipulated: propellers fore and aft, metal "wings" that crawl along the surface, down-facing lips that catch air and water somewhat like a popper. Surface-disturbing plugs are somewhat more versatile than poppers, since they can be fished quietly, as well as vigorously, and still have considerable action. Poppers may have the advantage when fish have to be attracted from some distance away, but more often the greater subtlety of the surface disturbers' action is effective. The "Jitterbug,"

FIGURE 7–3 A selection of surface plugs. *From the Left:* Hula Popper (Arbogast), Chugger Spook (Heddon), Jitterbug (Arbogast), Crazy Crawler (Heddon), Zara Spook (Heddon), Super Frog (Harrison-Hoge). (Photo by David Guiney)

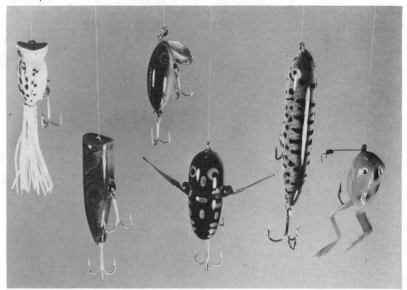

another Arbogast plug, is the favorite of this group of plugs. The "Crazy Crawler" from Heddon is another classic.

FLOATING-DIVING PLUGS

These floating-diving plugs float at rest on the surface, but dive when retrieved, an action that represents the behavior of a crippled or sick minnow. A plastic lip under the "chin" of the plug causes the diving action on retrieve. On some plugs, the depth of the dive can be modified by adjusting the plastic lip. On others, retrieve speed controls the depth; the harder you crank the reel handle, the deeper the plug goes. Even so, the floating-diving plug can't go much deeper than two or three feet; so they are used most in shallow water.

FIGURE 7–4
Three floating-diving plugs. *From the Left:* River Runt (Heddon), Wee Tad (Heddon), Floating-Diving Rapala (Rapala). (Photo by David Guiney)

Like the poppers and the surface-disturbers, the floating-diving plugs are fished along shorelines, weed beds, downed trees, and other "cover" where fish like to hide. They also work well when fished over submerged weed beds in lakes and impoundments. An excellent plug for this fishing is the "Rapala." This Scandinavian minnow imitation is one of the most popular of all plugs, and it's available in several configurations: a full floater, a floater-diver, and as a full sinker in several different weights.

SINKING PLUGS

Sinking plugs are heavier than water; therefore, they begin to sink immediately upon landing on the water. To fish them effectively, you have to learn the approximate sink rate of the plugs you use, and then experiment with different depths of retrieve. A common method of doing this is using the "countdown" method. After the plug hits the water and begins to sink, count "one thousand one, one thousand two, one thousand three . . ." and so on, beginning your retrieve at various depths until you get action. Then you can work the plug at the same

FIGURE 7–5 Deep-Running Plugs. *From the Left:* Sinking River Runt (Heddon), Devil Diver (Heddon), Arbogaster (Arbogast), Mud Bug (Arbogast). (Photo by David Guiney)

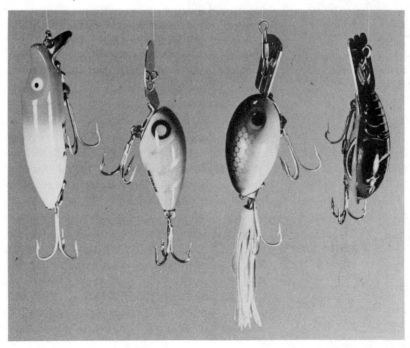

depth again by counting it down carefully. This method is particularly effective over a gradually sloping bottom where the fish may be holding at a particular depth.

Most sinking plugs have a wobbling, side-to-side action, and some set up vibrations in the water that their makers say are attractive to fish. Some have shot chambers in which weight may be added or removed to change the action, sink rate, and overall depth of the plug. The shot in these chambers may also rattle underwater as an added enticement. Finally, some deep diving plugs have a metal lip that forces them especially deep when you reel rapidly; you may get thirty feet deep or more with these "crankbaits," especially if you can make long casts that provide the lure with enough line to go really deep. For such plugs, you might find the steeply-geared, fast-retrieve reels desirable.

Sinking plugs are most effective when fished over bottom cover: deep weed beds, gravel bars, rock ledges, boulders, and such. Sinkers are also good fast water plugs, because their action is not as much affected by swift currents as is the action of floaters and floater-divers. The Heddon "River Runt" is a famous deep-running plug, although it is available in several other configurations, too.

Although you'll soon learn what to use in particular situations, a good rule of thumb for beginning pluggers is this: fish the floaters and floater-divers in shallow water early in the morning and in the late evening and the deep runners over cover in the bright midday hours.

When you shop for plugs, you'll find them available in a great many colors and finishes, some of them extremely lifelike. Old reliable colors and color combinations are red and white, black, yellow with black spots, and a green-and-yellow "frog" finish. If you start with a few plugs in these colors, you won't go wrong.

As far as weights are concerned, the range from three-eighth to three-quarter ounce is the "normal" range for freshwater fishing. Plugs in the one-sixteenth- to one-quarter-ounce range are highly effective, but they are too light for most beginners to cast except on lightweight spinning tackle. If you know already that you're interested in ultralight spinning, some plugs in this size range will increase your success. Large plugs may be several inches long and four ounces or more. The muskellunge angler needs them in such sizes, along with heavy bait-casting tackle to toss them with.

Plastic Lures

Soft plastic lures have been available since the 1940s, but have become widely popular only in the last couple of decades. You can find a plastic lure to imitate just about anything a fish might eat; crayfish, hellgrammites, minnows, snakes, grasshoppers, and grubs are just a few of the possibilities. Many of these lures are so realistic that you would think that they are devastatingly effective, but while all of them catch fish sometimes, only the plastic worm becomes a reliable "killer."

Plastic worms were around for some time before they made a big impact, because it took a while for anglers to discover the most effective way to fish them. The first fishermen to experiment with them fished them as they would a natural worm—with very little success. The successful method is representative of what no natural worm ever did: swimming along the bottom, slithering over rubble, weed beds, submerged tree limbs, and the like. Fished like this, the "worm" probably represents an eel or a small snake. Whatever the fish take it for, they *do* take it—and hard.

Rigging a plastic worm is a specialized technique, and there are several ways of doing it. Most involve using a sliding, tapered sinker, as shown in Figure 7–6. The sinker is threaded on the line, and the line is then tied to a special worm hook, usually one with an offset shank, as

FIGURE 7–6 Rigging a plastic worm

Sliding sinker already threaded on line above hook (note special curved shank worm hook); hook point is inserted into the middle of the worm and out the side.

The hook is pushed on through the worm until the hook eye is buried in the head of the worm. Then the shank is rotated to orient the point toward the worm body.

Point is imbedded in the worm, making the lure weedless. (Photos by David Guiney)

shown in the illustration. The point of the hook is started in the middle of the worm body and forced out the side of the worm a short distance back of the head. The hook is then turned one hundred eighty degrees and drawn through the worm until the eye and knot are buried; then the point is inserted back into the worm body. This rigging has several advantages. First, the worm is virtually snag-proof, especially when fished slowly; it can be drawn over and through all kinds of obstructions without hanging up. Secondly, the stiffness imparted by the hook to the front end of the worm enhances the slithering, wiggling action of the remainder. Finally, the sliding sinker allows a fish to pick up the worm without feeling much resistance.

A worm rig like this is usually fished slowly right on the bottom. The angler casts and watches the line intently as the worm sinks. If the line twitches or moves, you strike! Once the worm reaches the bottom, you can make it hop along very slowly by raising the rod, then dropping the tip and reeling up slack, raising the rod again, and so on. The worm is not actually reeled in, but "walked" across the bottom using the rod. The strike can occur at any portion of the sequence, but it is particularly likely when the worm falls as the rod tip is being dropped and slack reeled in. For this reason, most experienced worm fishermen "palm" their reels, with their left hand around the reel, thumb and first fingers lightly holding the line, feeling for any subtle tap that might signal a fish mouthing the worm. The angler must stay in contact with the worm at all times, and it takes experience to tell the difference between a fish and the feel of the bottom as the worm hops along. This need for "feel" is one reason why spinning outfits are not popular with worm fishermen; the placement of the reel under the rod makes it difficult to finger the line in this way while the other hand is reeling in slack.

At the first hint of a pickup, experienced worm anglers drop the rod tip, reel in all the slack line, and slam the hook home. The strike is so hard that they joke about "crossing the fish's eyes," and sometimes a small fish is launched into the air and right to the boat by the strike alone. This hard hook-setting strike is necessary to drive the hook point through the tough worm and into the fish. Often the hook is set three or four times for insurance. Both the force of the angler's strike and the need for precise "feel" dictate the characteristics of the "worm rod." It is stiff and thick, usually relatively short, and matched with lines from ten to eighteen pounds of test. Rubber worm artists take a lot of kidding about fishing with "broom handles" and "pool cues," but their brand of fishing requires such tools.

Worm fishing got its start on lakes and impoundments, particularly those harboring largemouth bass and walleyes, and such waters are still especially suited to the plastic bait. The most effective use of the worm requires knowledge of the bottom, and worm anglers use electronic depth finders, sonar units that print out contour maps of the bottom, and bottom maps of the lakes in their fishing. The fish are usually located over or in obstructions or snags, making the weedless quality of the plastic worm a major part of its appeal, along with the fact that the fish take it so consistently.

Worms are available in all shades of the rainbow, and worm addicts carry most of them; there's no telling what shade will be most effective on a particular day. Most experienced wormers would not be without black, red, blue, and purple worms, and if forced to choose one color for day-in-and-day-out fishing, many would choose purple. What natural food is imitated by a purple worm? Who knows? But if the fish take it, who cares? Surprisingly, the natural-colored worms are not particularly effective, although they look remarkably life-like. This fact supports the suspicion that plastic worms probably represent water snakes or eels rather than worms, at least in the fish's eyes.

Plastic worms are available in many lengths and sizes, and some are impregnated with scents and flavors that may lead the fish to hold on to them longer than they might otherwise and may even add to the initial attraction. They are usually used with hooks in sizes two to eight with sinkers of matching weight. Your tackle dealer or an experienced local angler can advise you on colors and sizes that are most effective in your area.

Spoons

Spoons are among the simplest of artificial lures, at least in appearance. They are elongated metal blades with hooks affixed at the rear, and the name derives from their superficial similarity to the common table

FIGURE 7–7 *Clockwise from Bottom:* Jig, spinnerbait, and spoon.

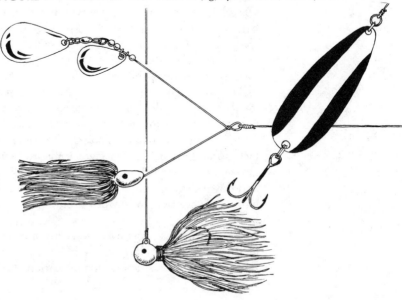

spoon. Spoons are designed with an intentional imbalance, so that they wobble when retrieved; this action throws erratic patterns of light flashes off the blade and creates vibrations as well.

Many spoons have a highly polished chrome or brass blade. Others, like the highly effective Dardevle, have an enamel finish. The appeal of a spoon is often enhanced by the addition of a piece of pork rind trailing from the hook, and some plastic worm anglers rig their baits on a spoon to add flash and glitter to their offering.

Spoons are good lures for beginners to fish with, because they will work with most any sort of retrieve and they are easy to cast. In fact, some beginning anglers get attracted to spoon fishing because of the casting practice spoons provide. Spoons cast almost as well as practice plugs. On the other hand, the best casting spoon might not be the most effective one in the water. The best casting spoons are usually narrow and heavy, presenting minimum air resistance. But that same spoon also offers little resistance to water, so it might not wobble as seductively as another spoon with a wider blade.

Typical spoons weigh from one-quarter to three-quarters ounce, suitable for use with light- to medium-weight spinning and spin-casting tackle. Bait-casting devotees can use spoons in that same weight range and on up. The ultralight spinning buff can get good results with tiny spoons in the one-sixteenth- to one-quarter-ounce range. Spoons for trolling or for big fish such as muskies may range up above the one-ounce level with blade lengths of three or four inches.

Jigs

Jigs are artificial lures that combine a lead head and a skirt of feathers, plastic, or animal hair. Jigs are typed according to the shape of the head: ball, oval, bullet, and so on. Many anglers make their own jigs by melting lead and pouring it into molds, forming the head of the jig around an offset-shank hook. On most jig hooks, the eye is offset down toward the plane of the point; when tied to the line, the point rides up, making the lure semi-weedless. At the same time, this position is not ideal for hooking the fish; therefore, the hook point on a jig must be kept needle sharp, or many takers will be missed.

Jigs may be hopped along the bottom much like a plastic worm. In fact, some bass fishermen favor a jig-and-worm combination. Jigs are also good lures to fish in snags, because they can be worked straight up and down through limbs and other obstructions. Jigs are also favorites with ice fishermen, who work them up and down through holes in the ice.

Like spoons, jigs cast well and sink quickly. Skirts of marabou feathers are particularly desirable on jigs, since the soft fibers will undulate with the slightest manipulation. Jigs come in all colors, even

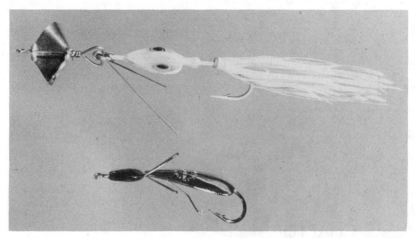

FIGURE 7–8 Two examples of the "buzzbait": Hawaiian Wiggler Sputterfuss (Arbogast), Weedwing (Harrison-Hoge). (Photo by David Guiney)

polka dots, but white, yellow, and black are probably the most popular. They can be purchased or made in the same weights as other artificials and can be fished with all kinds of tackle. Pork rind, plastic baits, even live minnows and worms can be added to jigs to increase their appeal. Simple as they are, jigs are extremely versatile. And since they are inexpensive compared to other lures (and cheaper yet if you make them yourself), your tackle box should always have a supply.

As you can see, the subject of artificial lures becomes a little less complicated when you consider the types rather than particular lures. You should probably resist the temptation to buy a lot of artificial lures to start with. Each type requires some special techniques, and until you learn those, you won't really benefit by having a large selection of lures. Get yourself a couple of lures in each category, paying particular attention to the sizes most suited to the type of tackle you want to fish with or the conditions that prevail in your area. Then spend your time learning how to fish your lures to maximum advantage. It's far better to carry only a few lures and fish them well than to have a whole box full that you don't know how to use. Plus, you'll save money by waiting to expand your lure supply until you know better the conditions under which you'll do most of your fishing.

CHAPTER 8

Fly Fishing

If you're like most people just getting into fishing, you may have a somewhat stereotyped concept of fly fishing—that it's practiced only by an elite corps of anglers who fish with six-hundred-dollar rods and mumble the Latin names of insects in their sleep. Like most stereotypes, this one is a great oversimplification.

Fly fishing *is* somewhat more complicated than many other types of angling, but it isn't especially difficult to learn nor is it restricted to members of an esoteric fraternity. Fly tackle, to be sure, can be quite expensive, and if you want to spend six hundred dollars on a fly rod, you not only can do so, but you will have several brands to choose from. However, you can also purchase a perfectly suitable outfit for thirty to fifty dollars, about the amount you'd spend for a spinning combination of comparable quality.

The real difference in fly fishing is not difficulty, but a greater opportunity for challenge. That's why fly anglers are such persistent evangelists for the method. They're having so much fun that they want to get all their friends involved.

And you can try fly fishing—now. While it's true that most fly anglers learned to fish first with other methods, that's not really significant, any more so than the fact that most people who drive cars first rode bicycles. You can start from scratch with fly fishing and do very well right from the beginning.

I know a lot of fly fishermen and have talked to many of them about what they find so fascinating about the sport. Based on those conversations and my own experience, I predict that you will probably like fly fishing if:

1. You love fishing, but hate waiting. Fly anglers don't need patience, because they're busy trying to make something happen, not waiting for it to happen. Fly fishing is active fishing.

2. You have an interest in nature, particularly the sort of ecological interest that focuses on the interrelationships among living things.

3. You care more about the experience of fishing than the fish itself. Most fly anglers practice catch-and-release fishing, because they recognize the benefits of it from a conservation standpoint and because they have learned that while catching fish is a necessary part of angling, it is not a sufficient satisfaction in itself.

4. You're easily bored and require continuing challenges. Once you get into fly fishing, you're unlikely ever to get out, because you'll never get to the end of the challenges it has to offer.

Fly fishing has a long heritage that goes back several centuries. It was born out of the need to imitate aquatic insects that make up a large part of the diet of game fish and cannot be used as live bait, because they are too small and fragile. This is still the major focus of fly fishing, but today the angler also imitates bait fish, land insects, crayfish, frogs—just about anything that lives in or happens into the water.

Fly Fishing Tackle

Fly fishing is based on a different principle from the other types of fishing that we have described so far. In each of those types, a lure or bait of significant weight is cast from the rod, and it pulls the line along behind it as it goes. In fly fishing, the flies used are nearly weightless and cannot be thrown through the air by themselves. In fly fishing, it is the line that is cast by the rod, and it carries the fly to the target.

If you've seen someone fly fishing, you've probably noted that the casting rhythm of the fly caster is different from that of the spinning angler or the bait caster. The fly angler's rod is usually longer, and his line is much thicker than the monofilament or braided line used in other

FIGURE 8–1 Fly casting is one of the most graceful sporting skills. Here's one of the best in action, Lefty Kreh. (Photo by Irv Swope)

types of fishing. All of these differences derive from the unique principle of fly fishing: casting the line instead of the lure.

Because of this special process of casting, you begin your selection of fly fishing equipment with the line. The line provides the casting weight, and, since that weight is spread out over the entire length of the line, line selection is a critical choice in matching equipment to the fishing to be done. Fly lines are rated according to the weight of the front thirty feet of line, the portion that is involved in an average cast, but all you need to know is the number associated with that weight. Once you decide on the number (weight) line you need for your fishing, then you can select a rod to match, choosing a length, action, and material that you prefer. Then you get a reel to hold the line and a selection of leaders, flies, and other accessories that you need.

CHOOSING LINE

How do you know what line you need? By deciding what conditions you will face most often and what types and sizes of flies you will be using most of the time. Table 8–1 will give you a breakdown.

As you might judge from the table, the most versatile lines are in the medium weights, and most beginners do well to select a six- or seven-weight line and a rod to match. If later you fish under more specialized conditions, that first outfit will serve you well enough to gain the needed experience to select the right tackle when you're ready for it.

The line should be a floating line and one of the good ones from Orvis, Cortland, Scientific Anglers, Berkley, or Shakespeare. You'll pay between fifteen and twenty-five dollars for a tapered fly line (more about

TABLE 8–1
Which Line to Use?

Designation	Line	Conditions	Fly Types and Sizes
Light	4–5	small streams, trout and pan-fish	wet and dry flies, #12–22, occasional small streamers and popping bugs
Medium	6–7	small and moderate size streams, farm ponds, small lakes, trout and bass	wets, dries, and nymphs, #8–16, streamers up to #4 medium-sized bugs
Heavy	8–9	big rivers, lakes, weedy or obstructed waters, bass, salmon, steelhead	large wets, nymphs #2–12, bushy bass bugs

taper in a moment), but this is no place to economize. A poor quality line won't cast well, won't float, just won't be satisfactory. No rod, however good, can compensate for a poor fly line.

Taper. Taper is something you should give some thought to. The taper of a line is any variation in diameter from one end of the line to the other. The least expensive lines have no taper at all and are called "level" lines; they offer adequate performance, but are not very good for long casts or for presenting a small fly with delicacy. The "double-taper" line is tapered down to a fine point at each end and level through the middle. Such a line is good for soft presentation of the fly and is economical, since the line can be reversed when one end becomes worn. The "weight-forward" line is tapered like the double-taper at the front end, but then narrows down into a small diameter "running line," which is designed to reduce drag in the rod guides during longer casts. The main disadvantage of the weight-forward lines is that they are not reversible.

A specialized variety of the weight-forward line is the "bug" taper. This line has the weight heavily concentrated near the front to aid in turning over relatively heavy, air-resistant bass bugs or other large flies. Delicacy is sacrificed with these lines, but it isn't important in the kind of fishing for which they are appropriate.

Whether you buy a level or tapered line depends on how you feel about fly fishing. If you feel as if you'll like fly fishing and will probably stick with it, go ahead and buy one of the tapered lines to start with; just about all serious fly anglers use them. If you're still in the "iffy" stage, you might just want to go with the level line. Be prepared to discard it quickly, though, if you get serious about fly fishing.

Level

Double Taper

Rocket Taper

Bug Taper

Salt Water Taper

Shooting Taper

FIGURE 8–2
Fly line tapers

Code. Line is designated according to a code system developed a few years ago by the American Fishing Tackle Manufacturers Association (AFTMA). The code uses numbers to indicate weight and letters to indicate the function of the line. Thus a line designated L7F is a level, seven-weight, floating line. One coded WF8S is a weight-forward line, eight-weight, sinking. A DT6F/S is a double-taper line, six-weight, with a sinking tip. This is a type of line that you might find useful if you need to get your flies deeper than you can with a standard floater. With the sink-tip, the first ten feet of the line sinks, and the remainder floats, making the line much easier to handle than a full sinking line. You can also get F/S lines in which the first twenty, or even the first thirty, feet sink. And there are a few conditions in which only a full sinking line will do the trick. Still, the one line you need for sure is the floating line. Even expert fly fishermen use floaters ninety percent of the time.

CHOOSING A ROD

Length. Once you have decided on your line, the biggest consideration in rod selection is length. Short rods (less than seven and a half feet) are too specialized for the beginner. They're harder to cast than longer rods, too. Very long rods (nine feet or more) are nice under a lot of conditions, but not comfortable to fish with unless they're made of graphite or boron, more expensive materials than the beginner ought to invest in.

A seven-and-a-half- or eight-foot rod, in good quality fiberglass, is about right for the beginner. I'd take the eight footer myself, because the extra six inches is often useful. You'll hear a lot about rod "action," and it can be an important consideration when you get to the point of investing in an expensive fly rod. Most fiberglass rods have a medium action, soft enough to be forgiving of the beginning fly caster and stiff enough to flick the moisture off a dry fly. Buy a glass rod from one of the good companies, such as Fenwick, Shakespeare, or Daiwa, and you'll get a good medium-action rod.

You can be sure that your chosen rod will cast well with your line by checking the manufacturer's designation on the rod shaft, right above the grip. The line weight (or, sometimes, weights) for which the rod is designed will be spelled out there. Don't overlook this information; it is the weight of the line that brings out the casting action of the rod. If they aren't matched properly, you'll have a hard time learning to cast.

Guides. In a fly rod, the guides are mounted, like the reel, on the underside of the blank. A rod should have at least as many guides as it is long in feet, and one more than that is okay, too. Some of today's rods come with small ceramic guides, but wire "snake" guides are still most common. Snake guides or not, the guide closest to the hand grip is a ring

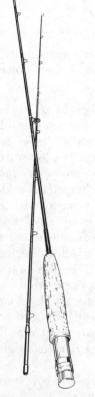

FIGURE 8–3 A typical fly rod

FIGURE 8–4 The line that each rod is designed to cast is marked on the rod shaft close to the handle grip. (Photo by David Guiney)

guide of some type, metal or ceramic. This is called the "stripper" guide, because it takes most of the line stress during casting. The other highly stressed guide is the "tip-top," which is the guide at the very tip of the rod.

SELECTING A REEL

Reel. The reel seat on a fly rod is located under the hand grip, so that the reel is below the angler's hand in casting. Some seats lock the reel on from the bottom up (up-locking) and some from the top down (down-locking). Some anglers have decided preferences, but it's a small matter in a first rod. Fly rod grips are almost always cork. Other fishermen may go for synthetic materials in their grips, but not fly fishermen. At least, not so far.

The reel for a fly outfit is one of the places where you can economize and still get a satisfactory product. Most popular is the "single-action" reel, as shown in several variations in Figure 8–5. In these reels, each turn of the handle equals one turn of the spool. A single-action reel can be expensive, but what you pay for in a costly reel for freshwater fly fishing is exotic materials and light weight. Good quality reels made of more mundane metals and plastic are available at fairly low prices, and you can do fine with those to start with (and to stay with, for that matter). Be sure that the reel that you buy will hold the line that you intend to fish with. Remember that a double taper line will require more spool area than a weight forward line in the same size, because it is thick for more of its length. Most reels specify the line sizes they will hold.

Automatic reels are widely advertised. I don't like them for several reasons. They're heavy, they don't usually have smooth drag systems, they don't have room for adequate backing behind the fly line. I'm

FIGURE 8–5 A group of single-action fly reels. *Clockwise from Top Left:* Cortland Graphite, Berkley 556, Cortland Crown, Hardy Marquis. (Photo by Katherine Lee)

seldom in situations where spooling line by pressing a lever is clearly superior to doing it by winding a handle. Some boat fishermen like them, though, because they slurp up line that might otherwise foul around obstacles in the boat. Suit yourself.

Multiplying fly reels have gears that produce several revolutions of the spool for each revolution of the handle. They are good for anglers who make repeated long casts or who fish for strong fish that might make a sudden run right at the angler, requiring rapid line recovery. But multipliers are heavier than single-action reels and much more expensive. You don't need one to get started.

Whatever type of reel you choose, be sure to get a model that has extra spools available. Even though you might not need one right away, at some point you'll want a sink-tip line and perhaps a full sinker, and extra spools provide a low-cost, low-bulk way of carrying them.

You will want some backing under your fly line, even though you might never encounter a fish large enough to take out all ninety feet of your fly line. The backing helps to build up the spool core, which allows you to retrieve more line with each turn of the handle. And backing also helps to avoid the kinks that result in the end of your line if you attach it directly to the bare spool. Any braided line can be used for backing (don't use monofilament!), but dacron is best, because it is small in diameter and it doesn't stretch or rot.

Leader. Line, rod, and reel. But you still need some other tackle, and the leader is one of the most important components. The leader provides the attachment between the fly and line, because the fly could not be tied directly to the bulky fly line. The leader also serves the function of separating the fly from the line, which is large enough to frighten fish, especially a floating line which casts a shadow on the bottom.

In order to accomplish these two purposes, the leader must be tapered; that is, it must be relatively large in diameter where it attaches to the fly line (the "butt") and quite small in the section to which the fly is tied (the "tippet"). The section in between, which gradually tapers down either through a chemical process or by a series of knotted strands, is called the "taper."

Leaders are sold by length and tippet size: for instance, seven-and-a-half feet, three X; nine feet, four X; and so forth. You can modify the length and size of a store leader by adding an additional strand; in other words, by adding a new tippet. Or you might need to replace the old tippet after changing flies a few times. In either case, you'll need a few spools of tippet material in addition to the complete leaders you buy. I'd recommend two leaders to start with: a seven- to eight-foot leader in three X and a nine-foot leader in four X. Add extra spools of tippet material in three, four, and five X.

Use either the blood knot or the surgeon's knot for adding tippet material. And use the tube knot to tie your leader butt to your fly line. Eventually you may start tying your own leaders from a kit. If you do, you'll save a little money and be able to custom-design your own leaders. But the store-bought kind are fine to start with, and most fly flingers use them for some applications long after they have become experienced fly fishermen.

Flies. You need something, of course, to tie on the tippet and present to the fish—flies. There are literally thousands of fly patterns to choose from, but they can be reduced to four basic groups:

1. Dry flies. These flies float on the surface of the water and represent either the adult stages of aquatic insects, such as the mayflies and caddisflies, or terrestrial (land) insects such as grasshoppers and ants.

   A variation of the dry fly is the bass bug, made of cork, wood, plastic, or deer hair. While bass bugs do not represent particular insects, they create a surface disturbance that attracts fish.

2. Wet flies. The oldest type of fly (two thousand years at least), the wet fly is fished under the surface. It may represent a drowned insect, an emerging insect, or a small fish.

99

FIGURE 8–6
Traditional dry flies (Photo by Katherine Lee)

3. Streamers and bucktails. These are specialized wet flies tied to imitate bait fish. Streamers are tied with feathers, bucktails with animal hair.

4. Nymphs. These, too, are specialized wet flies, which are tied to specifically represent the immature forms of aquatic insects, such as the mayflies, caddisflies, damselflies, dragonflies, and the like.

You may eventually become very interested in quite specific attempts to imitate particular species of insects at certain stages of their life cycles, but you don't have to get that specialized to catch fish. I'm going to recommend a few generalized flies, all classic patterns that you can easily order from catalogs or from local fly tiers. The size recommendations here are necessarily very general. Check with anglers in your own area before ordering, if possible.

FIGURE 8–7 Wet flies (Photo by Katherine Lee)

Dry flies: Adams, Light Cahill, Quill Gordon. Sizes 12 and 16. A floating ant pattern (the McMurray Ant is especially good) in sizes 14 and 20. Black is essential, cinnamon optional.

One of the good grasshopper patterns: Dave's Hopper, Jack's Hopper, Letort Hopper. Size 12. A couple of moderate sized bass bugs (2 and 4, for example) and some small plastic pan fish bugs.

Wet flies: Dark Hendrickson, Royal Coachman, Light Cahill. Size 12.

Streamers and Bucktails: Black-nosed Dace, Muddler Minnow, Black Marabou. Sizes 4 and 6.

Nymphs: Gold-Ribbed Hare's Ear, Muskrat. Sizes 8, 10, and 12.

FIGURE 8–8 A streamer

FIGURE 8–9 An artificial nymph

Most of these flies are classic trout patterns, but the hopper, the Adams, the Dark Hendrickson, and all of the streamers will catch bass,

101

FIGURE 8-10 Bass bugs (Photo by Katherine Lee)

as will, of course, the recommended bugs. That's a couple of dozen flies if you get the recommended sizes and a spare or two. If you want to go with the absolute minimum, get four flies: a #12 Adams, a #12 Royal Coachman wet fly, a #6 Muddler Minnow, and a #12 Gold-Ribbed Hare's Ear. With these four flies, you can catch fish anywhere in the country.

FIGURE 8–11 A dry fly of typical size and a "midge" (Photo by David Guiney)

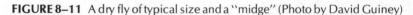

Fly Casting

To catch the fish, though, you've got to get the fly to them, and that process is intimidating to many beginners. It's true that fly casting is a little more difficult than, say, spin casting, but to call it hard would be an exaggeration. What's different about fly casting is that it requires some performances that seem *unnatural* to beginners. Once you've learned the skill, those movements seem like the most natural motions in the world, and you'll find that fly casting is one of the most rewarding skills you can learn.

Fly casting is governed by the fact that the line has weight and is cast by the rod. This means that while the *motions* involved are just like the casting motions used in other forms of casting, the *timing* of them is different. Since the fly line does not move through the air at high speed, the caster must learn to time his movements to make them most effective. Most poor fly casting is the result of employing the right motions at the wrong time.

If you'll review the casting instructions given for bait-casting, spinning, and spin casting, you'll note that in all three cases the actual power in the cast is applied in the zone between eleven o'clock and one o'clock on the imaginary clock face. It is in exactly that same area that power is applied in fly casting. The difference is a *pause* between the back cast and the forward cast, and the duration of that pause varies with the amount of line being cast. Learning to fly cast consists of practicing until you learn to accurately judge the pause between the back cast and the forward cast.

Begin by gripping the rod as shown in Figure 8–12. Note that the thumb is on top of the hand grip in the illustration. While some anglers cast with their thumb on the side of the grip, applying pressure with the thumb is the easiest method for stopping the rod when necessary and applying power when you need it. The thumb on top facilitates this process.

FIGURE 8–12 Casting with the fly rod. (Illustration courtesy Zebco/Brunswick)

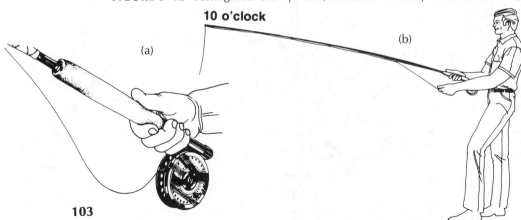

10 o'clock

(a)

(b)

103

Now get a mental picture of the proper movements for a good fly cast and the area in which they take place. Figure 8–12 will make this clear. As noted, the power of the cast is applied in the narrow zone between eleven and one o'clock; even though the rod may drift out of the power zone on either the back cast or the forward cast, that drift is *follow-through*. If power is applied outside this power zone between eleven and one o'clock, the cast will not be a good one.

The illustration also makes clear another point that you should keep in mind: Fly casting is done primarily with forearm movement rather than wrist movement. While the wrist does move during casting, this happens as a result of follow-through, not as a part of the power application. If you try to fly cast with your wrist, you will throw a wide, sloppy line, and you'll not be able to achieve distance or accuracy.

FIGURE 8–12 (*cont.*)

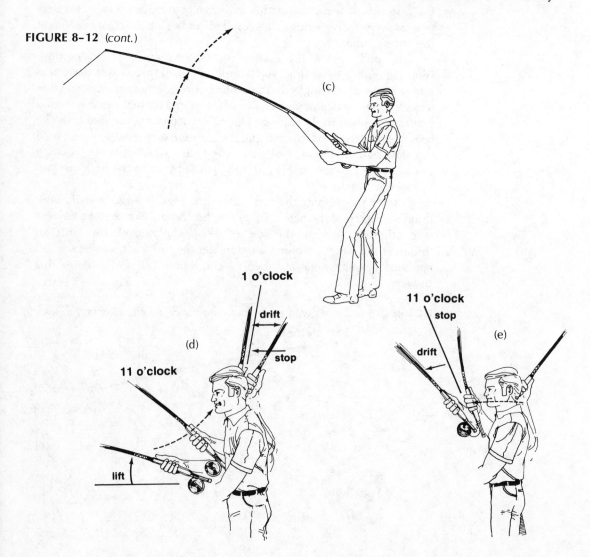

To begin your cast, strip out about twenty feet of line past the rod tip and stretch it out on the ground before you. With your rod gripped as shown in your right hand, take the slack line between the reel and the first guide in your left hand. Your line control hand is just as important to good casting as your rod hand. Now relax, letting most of your weight settle on the rod side leg.

Start the back cast by lifting the line from the ground with a smooth, even lift. Don't jerk the line; just raise the rod until all but the leader is clear of the surface; then accelerate your rod lift. What you want is a motion that starts slowly and smoothly and then accelerates strongly to the one o'clock position. At that point, you stop the rod quickly, as firmly as you can manage, as shown in Figure 8–13. This sends the line behind you in the backcast. When you stop the rod on the backcast, you form the "loop" in the fly line, which is so unique and essential to fly casting. The whole sequence is shown in Figure 8–13, so study it carefully.

Your natural tendency will be to start the rod forward immediately. You'll fear that the line will fall behind you, but it won't for a while yet. Turn your head and watch the line loop unroll on the backcast. Don't begin the forward cast until the line loop has almost completely unrolled. This is the "pause" that makes the difference between a fly cast and a mess of line around your ears.

FIGURE 8–13 Loop formation as a result of stopping the rod at the one o'clock and eleven o'clock positions. (Illustration courtesy Zebco/Brunswick)

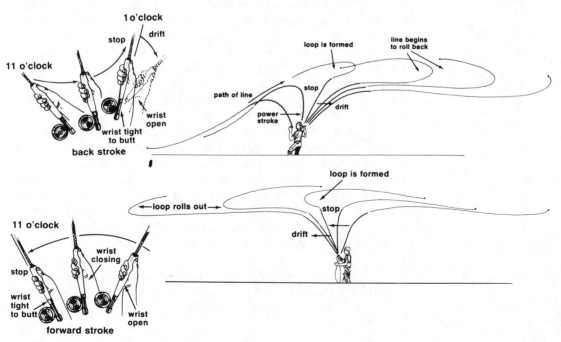

When the line is almost straight behind you, make the forward cast in the same way you made the back cast with a smooth, accelerating motion, stopping quickly at eleven o'clock. This stop creates the forward line loop that unrolls the line and carries the fly to the target. Note Figure 8–13.

Most beginners make a couple of characteristic errors when they first try to cast with a fly rod; I'll alert you to them. The most common error is excessive wrist movement, especially on the back cast. The second error, often the product of the first, is carrying the rod back too far, past the one o'clock position, which tends to drive the line *down* behind the caster rather than straight back. What both of these faults have in common is the application of power outside the proper power zone. You may often see an experienced caster, even a great caster, with his rod moving through a much wider arc than recommended here, but most of that movement is follow-through; the caster is not applying power outside of that power zone. Concentrate on keeping your rod in the power zone to start with, and you won't have so many bad habits to break later on.

One of the good ways to practice your casting is through *false casting,* in which the line is not allowed to fall, but is repeatedly moved through back cast to forward cast to back cast again. False casting is often used in fishing situations to measure the proper amount of line needed for a particular cast or for casting excess moisture off a dry fly. But it is good practice, too, because you can quickly see the changes in your cast as you apply power inside and outside the proper power zone. An ideal fly cast always has two characteristics: a straight line in the air and a tight line loop in both directions. As you practice your false casting, you'll see that this can only be produced by applying casting power in a narrow arc.

As with the other tackle, you'll often need to side cast with a fly rod. You should practice your basic cast in several planes—from sideways, to three-quarters, to straight up, as in the illustrations. Another cast you'll need to know is the roll cast, which makes it possible to cast in spite of obstacles behind the angler.

Keep in mind that in most cases you want to make a delicate cast that will allow the fly to alight with a minimum of disturbance. The way to produce such a cast is to aim high, so that the line unrolls a couple of feet above the water and then falls quietly to the surface, taking the fly and leader down with it. This sort of cast also tends to create a little slack in the leader so that when the fly lands it will float or drift freely with the current. A fly which does not follow the currents naturally is said by fly anglers to "drag," and drag usually alerts the fish to the unnaturalness of the fly.

We've only scratched the surface of fly fishing. There are a number of good books about it, and you'll probably find a course of instruction available to you, perhaps through a Federation of Fly Fishers or Trout Unlimited chapter in your area, at a local community college, or offered by a fly shop or fly tackle company. Since there is a lot to learn about fly fishing, taking a course like this is a good idea. And don't worry that taking a course or reading a couple of books will take the fun out of learning it for yourself. You can study fly fishing for a lifetime and not learn it all.

9

Fish: In General and In Particular

Fish are not like you and me. In fact, apart from being vertebrates, fish and humans have little in common. It may be that this dissimilarity has been one source of man's fascination with fish through the ages. Fish live in what to us is a mysterious, yet compelling, environment, and their behavior interests us because it is so different from our own. Fish and humans share a number of organs and systems, as the illustration in Figure 9–1 shows. But the systems of fish are usually simpler than those of people, and this is especially true of the nervous system.

General Characteristics

Although anglers often speak of fish as if they were intelligent, decision-making creatures, this is probably inaccurate. The brains of fish are not designed for pondering the meaning of life (or anything else, for that matter). It is true that fish can learn, but their learning is mechanical, and they do not accumulate a body of information from which they can draw when confronted with novel situations. The behavior of fish is governed largely by reflex and instinct rather than by rumination.

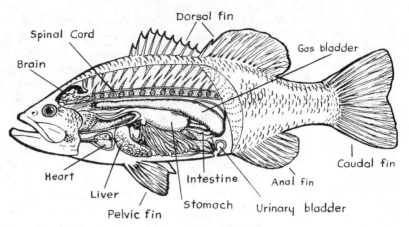

FIGURE 9–1 The anatomy of a fish

TEMPERATURE

One of the most important characteristics of fish is that they are cold-blooded organisms. Their body temperatures change with the temperature of the water in which they live, with resulting changes in their metabolism and activity level. Temperature variations control such activities as feeding, spawning, and migration, and the temperature of water also influences the levels of dissolved oxygen that the water can hold.

Water temperature is one of the most important influences on fishing success. You should carry a thermometer and use it often. You should take readings several times during the fishing day and at several different locations. You'll find that the water temperature varies with the season, time of day, air temperature, depth, and proximity to springs and feeder streams, among other variables. If you keep records, you will soon see a relationship between temperature and your fishing success, and you'll discover trends that will improve your future fishing. Most aquatic biologists would agree that water temperature has a greater influence on fish behavior than any other single variable. And, as you'll see when we get to the particulars of this chapter, the species vary in their temperature requirements and preferences. But first you will have to take other characteristics of fish into consideration.

MOTIVATION

The first rule of life is survival, and fish are no exceptions to this rule. They never stray far from a source of protection. In angler's jargon, this protection is called "cover." Cover might be depth; it might be a submerged weed bed, brush, a downed tree, or a rock ledge. In im-

109

poundments, the now-flooded contour of once-dry land provides all sorts of cover: old streambeds, roads, building foundations, fence rows, still-standing timber or stumps, just to suggest a few. Cover is so important that when fishing any large body of water, you should procure topographic maps of the bottom if possible. Also, you'll benefit from modern, sonar depth-finding gear that can give you a visual indication of the bottom contour. The most sophisticated of these devices will draw a picture of the bottom structure on a piece of paper and hand it to you! When you find cover, you usually find fish.

Keep in mind that different species of fish prefer different kinds of cover. Crappies like brush when they can find it, while largemouth bass prefer downed trees and lily pads. Smallmouth bass like rocks, and muskellunge like weed beds. And all these cover preferences are further influenced by factors such as temperature and the availability of food. It's the interaction of all these factors that make fishing so complicated and challenging.

VISION

Most fish can see from thirty to fifty feet in clear water. While this makes them nearsighted in a technical sense, they still have quite enough visual acuity to detect the approach of a careless angler. And since they can see much that is behind them as well as in front, careful stalking is required, especially in small stream fishing.

HEARING

While fish have ear structures, they do not have external sound-gathering organs like we do. What they have instead is the *lateral line*, a bundle of specialized nerve fibers that appear often as a dark stripe down the fish's side. The lateral line detects vibrations transmitted through the water. Fish are quite sensitive to underwater sounds, such as that made by a carelessly dropped anchor hitting bottom. They cannot hear sounds made above the surface unless something conducts these sounds into the water. Now you know why carpeting in boats is not just for luxury!

FEEDING HABITS

Fish do not feed continuously, and their feeding is determined to some degree by environmental conditions and by differences between species. Muskellunge, for example, are sight feeders that stalk their prey, so night fishing for them is not usually productive unless a bright moon is shining. Walleye, on the other hand, are largely nocturnal. They feed heavily at night, probably by detecting the vibrations made by the small fish they feed on, then closing in on them using their dark-adapted eyes.

Some fish, like the smallmouth bass, don't like the sun. When they feed in the daytime, they select shady areas. Others, yellow perch, for example, seem to like high noon and are often caught by the buckets on bright days.

Generally speaking, morning and evening are the best times to fish for most species. By fishing at these times, you can catch both the nocturnal and daytime feeders at the beginning or end of their forays, and the long shadows of dusk and dawn provide protection and security for the fish you're seeking (and for the prey they're seeking).

In Particular

Now let's move beyond the generalizations and look at specific fish and their habits and characteristics. These will just be thumbnail sketches, but hopefully they'll contain a few ideas you'll find useful. I considered many different methods of organizing the list and all seemed to create some confusion. So I've decided to use alphabetical order, based on common names.

ATLANTIC SALMON (*Salmo salar*)

"The king of fish, the fish of kings." The Atlantic salmon has earned that title through a combination of scarcity and superiority. It is a beautiful, courageous, strong fish, touched with the mystery and romance of salt water, and now gravely threatened by destruction of habitat and netting at sea.

Atlantic salmon are *anadromous* fish—that is, they are hatched in fresh water, swim to the sea to mature, and return to their native freshwater streams again to spawn. A few are "landlocked" salmon, presumably trapped by glaciers eons ago in freshwater lakes in New England. But it is the nature of the salmon to be migratory, to roam and fatten in the sea, and then to return to the stream of its origin to begin the cycle again.

Young salmon remain in fresh water from one to five years before yielding to the lure of salt water. Having gone to sea, a few come back to fresh water after only one year. Still immature, these fish, called *grilse*, weigh four to eight pounds and are considered by many veteran salmon anglers to be the gamest and strongest, pound for pound, of the species. True *salmon* have been at sea at least two years and usually run nine to

FIGURE 9–2 The Atlantic Salmon: most prized of all trophies. (Photo courtesy U.S. Fish and Wildlife Service)

twelve pounds. Three-year fish may weigh up to thirty pounds, and the rare fish with more than three years at sea may go up to fifty pounds.

Unlike Pacific salmon, Atlantic salmon do not necessarily die after spawning, and an individual fish may spawn two or three times. Fish returning from the sea to spawn do not feed, so anglers must appeal to other motives to entice them to strike. This is one reason that salmon flies are so colorful and complicated; since no one knows why salmon strike them, their design is more a matter of art than science.

The damming and pollution of rivers has greatly reduced the population of Atlantic salmon. Although some progress is being made in a few of the New England states that once had strong salmon runs, Maine remains the only state with extensive fishing for Atlantic salmon. However, Atlantic salmon can be fished in Canada's maritime provinces, and in Iceland, Norway, England, Ireland, and Scotland. Fly fishing is the preferred method; in many countries and provinces, no other method is legal. Salmon may be enticed to take a dry fly under certain conditions, but sunken patterns are more commonly used. A seven-weight fly outfit would be considered light, a nine-weight more typical. Rods are usually long, nine feet or more, because hundreds of long casts may be required before the fish can be enticed to strike. Backing is important, because the salmon is capable of making long runs. Two hundred yards of twenty- to thirty-pound dacron is recommended.

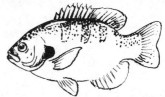

BLUEGILL (*Lepomis macrochirus*)

That the lordly Atlantic salmon should be followed by the lowly bluegill seems slightly absurd, but the alphabet goes from A right to B every time you try it. And since many an Atlantic salmon devotee started his angling career with a farm pond bluegill, the juxtaposition might not be so nonsensical after all.

The bluegill is the pan fish personified. Scrappy, tasty, ready to feed on most anything offered, bluegills have been the childhood quarry of many an angler. They are fish of quiet water, preferring ponds and impoundments; in rivers, they seek the slowest current. Bluegills vary considerably in color from one habitat to another. The dark blue gill flap (it looks black on most specimens) is the identifying characteristic.

In most bluegill waters, spring fishing begins in earnest when the water warms to sixty degrees Fahrenheit. Spawning begins between sixty-five and seventy degrees. Bluegills will take live bait, flies, small spinners, and spoons. Popping bugs in small sizes (6 to 12) will work, and a black sponge rubber spider is a deadly bluegill fly.

BROOK TROUT (*Salvelinus fontinalis*)

The brook trout is not actually a trout at all, but a char, a relative of the lake trout. True trouts are members of the *Salmo* genus, cousins of the Atlantic salmon. No matter, the "brookie" is still one of the favorite game fish of American anglers.

The brook trout is one of the most vulnerable of fish, requiring water no warmer than fifty-five to seventy degrees and pristine stream conditions. It cannot stand the eighty-degree temperatures that many of today's "trout" streams reach in late summer. "Native" fish are found in high mountain streams throughout much of the East Coast, but most of them grow to be no more than a few inches long, since the high streams are not very fertile in producing insect life and other food the fish need to grow large. Brook trout in such circumstances are easy to catch if you can get close enough. They are not particular in their choice of food, but are extremely shy, ready to bolt from a shadow or a waving rod. Fishing under such conditions is challenging, even if the "trophy" might be eight inches long!

Brook trout are fall spawners, and they require cold, spring-fed water and clean gravel bottoms. Logging ruins brook trout habitat by creating siltation that makes successful reproduction impossible. Spawning brook trout often run up into small tributaries of the main stream to spawn. In lakes, they will choose shallow areas for spawning if no tributaries are available.

Where brook trout have access to salt water, a few will run to the sea; these fish are called "salters." Brook trout grow large in Canada, but most United States fish are relatively small, with the exception of a few productive areas in the northern states. Many of the hatchery fish released in put-and-take trout streams are brook trout, but these are genetically far removed from their wild ancestors.

Brook trout are not as discriminating in their feeding as the true trouts. They will take live bait of all kinds, prepared baits like cheese and canned corn, lures, spinners, and flies, including the bright patterns that don't resemble any natural food.

BROWN TROUT (*Salmo trutta*)

The brown trout is the wiliest of the trouts and the fly angler's favorite quarry. Native to Europe, the brown was introduced into North America in 1883. It was at first despised by American anglers, because it was difficult to catch in comparison to the native brook trout they were used to. But as anglers became more sophisticated, the wariness of the brown trout became more appreciated. The brown is also a more adaptable fish than the brook trout; it can stand somewhat higher water temperatures and does not require such pristine stream conditions.

The brown trout prefers water temperatures of fifty-five to sixty-two degrees Fahrenheit and feeds most heavily under such conditions. That these temperatures coincide with the greatest insect activity is no accident. Brown trout are insect feeders and can become highly selective to a particular insect when large numbers are present. This quality helps to endear the brown trout to the fly fisherman who wants as challenging a quarry as possible.

After reaching twelve to fifteen inches, brown trout rely more and more on small fish for the bulk of their diet, although they continue to take insects when they are available in good quantity. Even large browns will rise to floating flies during heavy emergences of aquatic insects.

Really big browns tend to become nocturnal feeders, particularly when they live in relatively small streams. Although anything over three pounds is a big brown in most places, stream browns can range up to ten pounds or so, and thirty-pound fish are sometimes caught in particularly rich river or lake environments. Browns can be taken on bait and hardware, especially during the high and cloudy water conditions that often prevail in early spring. But the brown trout is ideally a fly fish; if you want to appreciate the brown trout to the fullest, seek it with the fly rod.

CARP (*Cyprinus carpio*)

The carp is a fish that practically no one feels neutral about. To fans, the carp is a tasty fish that is relatively easy to catch, puts up a good, if not spectacular, fight, and is at least attractive, if not beautiful. To detractors, the carp is a trash fish, grotesque in appearance; they argue that it overpopulates our streams, thriving on the pollution and siltation that defiles the habitat for more desirable game fish. The controversy probably tells as much about the fishermen as the fish.

The carp is not a native fish but was imported from Europe in 1876. Even proponents would probably agree that importing the carp was a bad idea, at least when viewed in retrospect. Carp are prolific breeders and often crowd out more desirable species. Moreover, they are bottom feeders and their rooting muddies the water, making the habitat less desirable for fish that require clean water and clear bottoms to thrive.

To this controversy the carp pays not the least attention. It prefers slow streams or shallow lakes and ponds. Silt bottoms and muddy water suit the carp fine. High water temperatures and high organic loads in the stream are no problem. Carp can reach ten pounds in most streams, and sixty- and seventy-pound fish have been caught. One reason carp get so big is that they live for a long time, at least for a fish—twenty to twenty-five years.

Not all cultures take the dim view of the carp that many Americans do. They are highly prized game fish in Europe, and, in the Orient, carp are considered decorations and cultivated like flowers.

Dough balls are probably the most widely used bait for carp. Like the catfish, carp have barbules outside their mouths, and these barbules have taste buds on them. Therefore, carp can taste food without ingesting it, so that carp fanciers try to perfect recipes that they think will present the carp with a satisfactory taste sensation.

Carp can also be taken on live bait, such as minnows and worms, and they often feed on the immature forms of aquatic insects. When carp are spotted feeding on insect larvae, the fly flinger can often induce one to take an artificial nymph or small streamer. My friend Ben Schley has caught a few on dry flies. A carp on a fly rod is something like a hog on ice—not pretty, but exciting and unpredictable.

CHANNEL CATFISH (*Ictalurus punctatus*)

Of the many species of catfish in the United States, the channel "cat" is probably the most popular with anglers. It prefers clearer water than some other members of the catfish family, takes artificial lures frequently, and feeds by sight, as well as by taste and feel.

Like other catfish, the channel catfish has external barbules that combine taste, smell, and touch. It also has a deeply forked tail, which is a distinguishing feature. Ranging from Canada to Mexico, the channel catfish likes flowing rivers and clear lakes and prefers bottoms without silt. The average river fish runs to a couple of pounds, but a ten-pound channel "cat" is no trophy in most waters, and specimens up to sixty pounds have been landed.

The channel catfish is a fine food fish and is widely grown commercially, along with the blue and white catfishes. Since catfish can turn feed into flesh far more efficiently than cattle or poultry, many scientists think that catfish farming can someday contribute greatly to feeding the world's population.

Channel catfish respond well to bait fishing. A particularly effective way to fish for them is to cut strips of flesh from another fish (including another catfish!) for bait. Chicken livers and shrimp are good bait. They also will take minnows (dead or alive), crayfish, worms, and whatever else you have handy. Corn, dough balls, cheese, and commercial catfish baits take large numbers of fish. Channel cats can also be taken on spinners, spoons, deep running plugs, and even flies. Night fishing is often productive.

CRAPPIE
(BLACK CRAPPIE—*Pomoxis nigromaculatus*; WHITE CRAPPIE—*P. annularis*)

The two species of crappie are so nearly alike that they can be treated as one here. Crappies are found throughout the East and Midwest and the upper Western states. They are school fish and breed prolifically, so they are often taken in large numbers. They are considered a fine eating fish, although they have many tiny bones.

Crappies are easiest to catch during spring spawning. Water temperatures of sixty to sixty-five degrees bring on the spawning urge, and fish are taken both before and after the actual spawning period. While on the spawning beds, crappies are very vulnerable to small minnows or minnow imitations, which they probably interpret as invaders of the nest.

116   At other times of the year, crappies are harder to locate, but they

will usually be found close to cover, particularly brush. Stream crappies love downed trees, and impoundment fish like to lurk in the branches of submerged trees when possible. Although most crappies are not large, they can put up a good struggle by turning their flat sides toward the resistance of the rod. They are challenging to fish for, too, because they take the bait or lure delicately and have paper-thin mouths; if they are not played carefully, the hook will often tear out or fall out before the crappie can be landed.

Lively small minnows are the best year-round crappie bait. Artificial nymphs and small streamers will score for the fly angler, and small spinners and spinner-fly combinations for the fisher who prefers the spinning rod.

CUTTHROAT TROUT (*Salmo clarki*)

The cutthroat trout is a fish of the western United States. A relative of the rainbow trout with which it sometimes shares habitat, the cutthroat is distinguished by a red slash on the lower jaw.

Yellowstone Park has fine cutthroat fishing, as does Idaho's Snake River. Cutthroats are winter and spring spawners. They are relatively easy to catch compared to other trouts. Heavy fishing pressure often

FIGURE 9–3 Cutthroat trout are found in some of the most beautiful parts of the country. Here an angler on horseback plays a cutthroat. (Photo courtesy U.S. Fish and Wildlife Service. Photo by Richard Blades)

must be controlled by special regulations to avoid reducing the population of cutthroats too drastically.

Although cutthroats are easy to take with spinners and live bait, waters where they are found are often limited to fly fishing only.

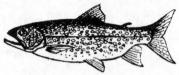

LAKE TROUT (*Salvelinus namaycush*)

Like the brook trout, the lake trout is not properly a trout at all, but a char. As the name indicates, the lake trout is a deep-water fish, seldom found in streams, except in rivers that adjoin the deep lakes where they spend most of their time.

The "laker" is a fish of Canada and the northern United States, particularly in "shield" lakes formed by glacial action. These lakes are mostly rock bottomed and relatively barren; the lake trout may share them with walleyes and smallmouth bass, but usually there will not be large concentrations of any of these species present.

Smaller fish are the usual fare of the lake trout, especially the cisco. Fishing for lake trout requires specialized equipment, including electronic depth finders. Since lake trout are often located at extreme depths, special downrigger trolling rigs are used. These depth-probing outfits usually incorporate a very heavy sinker and a metal line to which the actual fish line is attached. The downrigger takes the lure down to a productive level, and when the fish strikes, the line is released by a special clip so that the fish can be fought from the rod unimpeded by the downrigger. Lakers are often caught and brought up from such depths that releasing them is impractical; they die anyway from the sudden change in pressure.

Temperature is the key to locating these fish. They avoid water cooler than forty-three degrees or warmer than fifty-six; fifty-two is ideal. Many boats designed for laker fishing have digital readout temperature probes that give temperature and depth readings as they are lowered toward the bottom.

Lake trout spawn in fall, often in very deep water. In spring they may be found in tributary rivers for a short period, and here they will be vulnerable to flies and spinners. Most of the time, however, they are taken on live bait or large spoons, spinners, and lures trolled deep.

LARGEMOUTH BASS
(*Micropterus salmoides*)

The largemouth bass is the most popular gamefish in the United States, bar none. Improved techniques and equipment for largemouth fishing

FIGURE 9–4 Spinning angler demonstrates lip-landing technique on large-mouth bass. (Photo courtesy U.S. Fish and Wildlife Service. Photo by Dr. F. Eugene Hester)

have greatly expanded the interest in this fish in recent years, and its favor with anglers has been growing spectacularly.

The largemouth bass is similar to the smallmouth in appearance, but a careful eye can distinguish the two at a glance. The jaw of the largemouth comes to the rear of an imaginary line drawn vertically through the center of the eye while the smallmouth's jaw does not extend so far back. The dorsal fin on the largemouth is almost completely separated into two; on the smallmouth the connection is obvious. And the largemouth shows a preponderance of horizontal markings, particularly a dark side stripe in small fish, while the smallmouth shows a barring pattern in which most of the markings are vertical.

The two species prefer slightly different habitats, although they often overlap in their ranges. The smallmouth likes rocky, swift streams and cool lakes, while the largemouth prefers slower, warmer waters, likes weeds, and thrives in large impoundments. The largemouth is now found in all of the contiguous states, and its adaptability is one reason for this wide distribution.

Largemouth bass are spring spawners, beginning to spawn when the water warms to the mid-sixties. Many large bass are taken during spawning time when the introduction of a lure or bait into the nest can arouse the bedding fish to furious attack.

After spawning, largemouth bass prefer water temperatures in the high sixties and seventies, and they can tolerate higher temperatures. They like to hide around weed beds, deadfalls, lily pads, and other cover, and popping bugs and topwater plugs delivered to such areas can score well, particularly in morning and evening.

During the bright daylight hours, bass spend most of their time in deeper water. They particularly like sharp dropoffs and depressions. Here they will take live bait and lures of all descriptions. The plastic worm is the number one bass lure, with the spinner close behind, but large and lively shiners are the best bet for the trophy hunter. Fly fishing with streamers and popping bugs is also effective, especially in the spring and fall when the fish are cruising shallow water looking for food.

MUSKELLUNGE (*Esox masquinongy*)

If fish were evaluated by mystique, the "musky" would win hands down. It is a mysterious, unpredictable, maddening quarry, damnably difficult to catch. It is also a large, toothy, vicious predator, strong enough in battle to require the heaviest of freshwater tackle.

The muskellunge is the largest of the pike family. It is easily confused with the Northern Pike, but the muskellunge has no scales on the lower half of the cheek and gill cover. And muskellunge are either barred or covered with dark spots while the pike has light spots. Muskies were once largely limited to the area of the United States–Canada border, but they've been widely planted in man-made lakes, even in the South.

Muskellunge prefer quiet water, weed beds, and shallow areas with deep water nearby. They don't move much, although they will go deep in lakes in the summer. The musky is a pure predator. It feeds only on live, lively quarry, which it stalks ominously, striking with a snake-like slash. Muskies don't feed often; many studies indicate that they tend to eat big meals and then wait until digestion is complete before feeding again.

Anglers dedicated to fishing for these fish usually seek them with big suckers or huge surface or shallow running lures. Mid-morning fishing is most productive in most areas. Heavy spinning or bait-casting tackle is required, both to deliver the bait or lure and to fight the fish after the hookup. But the hookups can be few and far between. Dedicated musky anglers can wait for years between fish and then hit a streak where they catch several in a short period. Persistence is the name of the game. And cool nerves are desirable, too. A musky will often follow a lure right up to the boat before taking it—or turning away and sinking back out of sight.

NORTHERN PIKE (*Esox lucius*)

The pike is closely related to the muskellunge and, like the musky, was once mostly limited to the northern United States and Canada. It has now been introduced to the South and West. Like the other members of the pike family, the Northern is a long, toothy fish with a body shading from dark olive over the back to a white belly. Spots are yellow and elongated.

Pike spawn in the spring as soon as the ice melts. After spawning they go on to feed, and fishing is good. When water temperatures reach sixty-five or so, the fish go deep and don't feed at night under ordinary circumstances. A number of studies show that pike tend to be morning feeders, eating "breakfast" at about the same time most people do. They will eat anything. Plugs, spinners, big spoons, large streamer flies, and live bait are all good for pike fishing. Although pike as large as forty pounds have been caught, a twenty-pounder is considered a fine fish.

PACIFIC SALMON
(*genus Oncorhynchus*)

There are five species of Pacific salmon: chinook (*O. tshawytscha*), coho (*O. kisutch*), sockeye (*O. nerka*), pink (*O. gorbusha*), and cherry (*O. masou*). The chinook, coho, and sockeye have all been introduced successfully into the Great Lakes, but the majority of Pacific salmon remain West Coast natives, ranging the ocean and the coastal rivers from California to Alaska.

Hatched in fresh water, Pacific salmon go to sea after several months to a year or more, depending on the species. They remain in the Pacific from two to seven or eight years and they return to spawn in freshwater streams. Unlike Atlantic salmon, the Pacific fish die after spawning.

Pacific salmon are generally silver with blue or olive backs and

FIGURE 9–5 This Pacific Salmon shows the hook jaw characteristic of males ready for spawning. (Photo courtesy U.S. Fish and Wildlife Service. Photo by G. Atwell)

dark spots, except during the spawning season, when their colors may become bright reds, oranges, and yellows. The males develop hooked lower and upper jaws prior to reproduction.

Sport anglers troll for returning fish in the estuaries and bays and cast spinners, flies, and lures for them in the freshwater streams. Pacific salmon are among the best table fish. Many anglers smoke their salmon, and private canneries also provide for the preservation of the angler's catch.

Pacific salmon are the most important commercial fish in the United States. Many are harvested at sea, but a number of canning companies are now "farming" these salmon, breeding their own fish in private hatcheries and then releasing them to run to sea, knowing that the fish will eventually return right to the processing plant after fattening in the Pacific.

PUMPKINSEED (*Lepomis gibbosus*)

The ubiquitous pumpkinseed is one of the most widely distributed members of the sunfish family. Among the most colorful of the pan fish, it is distinguished by a black gill cover with a red or orange spot on the tip and by wavy, blue lines radiating back from the eyes.

Pumpkinseeds are reckless feeders, perfect for teaching kids to fish. They like still water and plants for a habitat and bite readily on garden worms, grubs, tiny spinners, and flies, particularly wet flies that resemble aquatic insects. Like others in this genus (bluegills, for example), pumpkinseeds are spring spawners, building round nests in the shallow water when the temperature reaches near seventy degrees. Filleted and fried, a "mess" of pumpkinseeds is hard to beat.

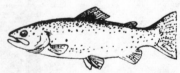

RAINBOW TROUT (*Salmo gairdneri*)

The rainbow is the native American among the true trouts, originally limited to the Rocky Mountain area. Hatchery strains have now been planted all over the United States.

There are many color variations in rainbow strains, with the majority showing the pink or red side stripe that is the basis for the name. Some fish, however, are primarily silver with dark spots. The rainbow is a spring spawner, requiring flowing water and clean bottom gravel for successful reproduction. When rainbows are planted in lakes, they will attempt to run into tributary streams to spawn.

Rainbows feed most actively when temperatures are in the fifty-five- to sixty-degree range. The fish can tolerate temperatures from the mid-thirties into the low eighties for short periods, so they can be planted in streams too warm for the native brook trout.

Rainbow trout are free-rising fish, readily taken on dry flies, as well as subsurface imitations. When hooked, they are acrobatic fighters, much more likely to jump than brown trout. Spinners, spoons, and live bait also produce well. Hatchery rainbows are suckers for cheese balls, canned corn, and worms, especially when fishing can begin shortly after the fish are planted.

In many Western streams, the rainbows are migratory, running to salt water or into big lakes. Returning as mature fish, they are called *steelhead,* and they are among the most popular game fish in the country. Like the Pacific salmon, steelhead strains have been planted in the Midwest, and a number of the Great Lakes now have reliable steelhead fishing, both in the lakes themselves and in tributaries.

Unlike most other anadromous fish, steelhead do feed during migration, and anglers fish for them with live bait, spinners, sacks of salmon eggs, and "cherry bobbers," artificial lures made to resemble a cluster of salmon eggs. Fly fishing is also effective, and most anglers use bright wet patterns similar to Atlantic salmon flies.

Steelhead runs are under way most months of the year in one drainage basin or another. The fish that come in during summer are immature and will not spawn immediately, but winter fish are ready for spawning when they return from the salt.

REDBREAST SUNFISH
(*Lepomis auritus*)

Another of the prolific *Lepomis* genus, the redbreast roams most warm rivers on the Atlantic seaboard. The redbreast likes stronger currents than most sunfish and will often be found in the same habitat with smallmouth bass, although the redbreast will occupy the slower areas of the stream. The redbreast is a brightly colored fish, especially in spring spawning array, and is distinguished by a gill flap that is black, like the bluegill's, but long and narrow.

Spawning in the spring begins when water temperatures climb to sixty-eight to seventy degrees. Spawning fish are easy pickings, but then the redbreast is not a difficult fish to catch at any time. They will take small lures and flies, taking surface lures and bugs more readily than most other pan fish except the bluegill. They tend to hug the shoreline, especially where weed beds and other cover are available. Since they like some current, redbreasts are more likely to be found on the outside bend of river curves than on the inside, other conditions being equal.

Small popping bugs will take a lot of redbreasts in the evening, as will sponge rubber spiders. Worms and grubs fished with a bobber will catch them most anytime.

ROCK BASS (*Ambloplites rupestris*)

The rock bass is somewhat misnamed. For one thing, it is not a bass, but a member of the sunfish family. For another, the fish is not a lover of rocks, at least not in comparison to the smallmouth bass, a fish for which the term "rock bass" would really be appropriate. The rock bass prefers quiet, protected waters, and in streams will be found where structural features have broken the current's flow to some degree.

The distinguishing feature of this fish is the dark red eye. It is often called a "redeye bass" and is known as the "goggle-eye" or "goggle-eye perch," especially in the South.

Although the rock bass is a sunfish, it has a larger mouth than most of the other members of the sunfish family, so it can be taken on larger hooks and lures. In fact, anglers fishing for the larger species, such as the true basses, often catch goggle-eyes. Ordinarily the rock bass is not a large fish, nor is it a spirited fighter compared to the true basses. But the rock bass is not moody, and can often be caught when more desirable species will not cooperate.

Rock bass prefer gravel bottoms, but will accept mud bottoms, if other factors are favorable. They feed not only on insect larvae, but also on larger food, especially minnows and small crayfish. They often hit small popping bugs and surface plugs, and gaudy wet flies and fly-and-spinner combinations can score well. The live bait angler can catch lots of redeye bass by fishing mayfly and stonefly larvae on light-wire hooks. And worms and grubs fished with a bobber will score with this accommodating fish.

SHAD (*Alosa genus*)

There are two species of shad of interest to anglers: the hickory shad (*A. mediocris*) and the American shad (*A. sapidissima*). The American shad is the larger of the two, running from two to ten or twelve pounds; the hickory averages two or three pounds, with a five-pounder a rare trophy. Both shads have gray-green backs shading to silver sides and deeply forked tails. They are related to the herrings with whom they share some freshwater streams.

Both species of shad are anadromous, hatching in fresh water and then running to sea where they mature. They are most often sought by sport fishermen when returning to freshwater streams to spawn. Baked shad is a delicacy, and the roe taken from ripe females is prized in gourmet circles. And since the fighting spirit of the shad has led to its nickname as "the poor man's salmon," there is no shortage of anglers interested in fishing during the shad runs.

Like most anadromous fish, shad evidently do not feed when returning to fresh water, but they can be goaded into striking small bright lures. The favorite is the shad dart, a small jig with bright feathers or hair, which is fished deep, usually with spinning tackle. Fly anglers use bright little streamer flies, often weighted with chain-bead eyes to get them down to where the fish are. Sink-tip or sinking lines are also often necessary. Like salmon and steelhead, shad will often stack up in pools and hold for some time before moving on upstream. In circumstances like this, shad can often be teased into striking by repeated casts that swing the dart or fly right past their noses.

Small spinners can also be effective during shad runs, and spoons and large spinners may also be trolled for the fish while they are in bays or large river mouths awaiting the warming temperatures that will draw them into the small streams where spawning takes place. Unlike most anadromous fish, shad do not always return to their native streams.

Originally an Atlantic fish, American shad were introduced into California in the late 19th century, and there are now good runs established in many Western rivers. A number of Atlantic Coast streams, though, have suffered declines or actual elimination of shad populations.

SMALLMOUTH BASS
(*Micropterus dolomieui*)

The smallmouth bass is distinguished from the largemouth by a jaw that does not extend past the midpoint of the eye and a dorsal fin that is not so deeply notched. The original Midwestern, Eastern, and southern Canadian range of the smallmouth has been greatly extended, thanks in part to the expansion of railroads in the late 1800s. Railroad men planted smallmouth bass in some of their now-famous homes, including the Potomac River.

Smallmouths prefer cooler and swifter water than do largemouths, and they favor rocky bottoms, particularly "rubble" bottoms featuring rocks the size of a cannonball and larger. They also frequent weed beds, especially those close to deep water.

Spring feeding begins in earnest when the water temperature reaches fifty-eight to sixty degrees. Smallmouths feed heavily just before spawning and are very vulnerable to anglers then. Spawning starts when the temperature climbs into the low sixties. After spawning, the male fish guard the nest and may often be goaded into striking by casting a lure or live minnow into the nesting area.

Smallmouth bass are more cautious than largemouths and more difficult to catch most of the time. Careless, noisy anglers don't catch many, particularly under low water conditions. When hooked, smallmouths almost always jump and are so strong for their size that they are widely regarded as the gamest of freshwater fish.

Live bait works well for smallmouth; live minnows, crayfish and hellgrammites are the most effective of the natural baits. Spinners and plugs score well, too. In fact, the smallmouth is a wonderful fly rod fish. It feeds freely on insects and can be taken on big nymphs, streamers, and even dry flies. Popping bugs are good, but they need not be large (#4 is about right) and should be fished with more subtlety than in largemouth bugging. Loud pops and gurgles may frighten the smallmouth away, but steady movement with erratic motions thrown in will usually produce action.

Smallmouth bass dislike bright sunlight and will feed in the shadows at midday, if they feed at all. Morning and evening offer the best action once summer arrives. In the fall, another feeding binge occurs as the fish put on weight for winter. October is a wonderful fishing month in most of the smallmouth's range.

STRIPED BASS (*Morone saxatilis*)

Originally a coastal fish, the striped bass was once important to freshwater anglers only when it ran into freshwater streams to spawn. Now, however, both natural striped bass and a hybrid fish (a striper-white bass cross) have been introduced into freshwater impoundments where they provide superb fishing.

Striped bass grow large, in part because they are a long-lived fish. Twenty- and thirty-pound fish are often caught, and a fifty-pounder is occasionally brought to net.

Saltwater stripers (called "rockfish" by some) run into coastal streams to spawn in the spring. Water temperatures of fifty-five to sixty degrees will bring them in, and the fish prefer to spawn in fast water, usually just below the "fall line" rapids of Eastern rivers. In fact, reproduction is not usually successful in quiet water, so striper populations in many impoundments have to be replenished by regular stockings. The hybrid fish, of course, cannot reproduce, so stockings are also required where they have been planted.

The striper is a heavy feeder and eats a wide variety of food. They rely particularly on smaller fish for their diet, and they respond well to live minnows and other forage fish, as well as to lures and flies that represent them. Gizzard shad are a staple food of the striper in many lakes.

Lake fish are caught by trolling deep running lures and by still fishing with live bait. Stripers sometimes feed on the surface after herding a school of bait fish to the top; when they do, popping bugs and streamers can score heavily, as can top-water plugs. Experienced striper anglers look for wheeling birds above the surface (they feed on the bait fish, too), then race at top speed to the area.

WALLEYE (*Stizostedion vitreum vitreum*)

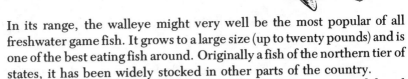

In its range, the walleye might very well be the most popular of all freshwater game fish. It grows to a large size (up to twenty pounds) and is one of the best eating fish around. Originally a fish of the northern tier of states, it has been widely stocked in other parts of the country.

The walleye is an elongated fish with two clearly separated dorsal fins. Large luminous eyes are a distinguishing feature, as is a white or silver spot on the bottom of the tail, a mark which distinguishes the walleye from the sauger, a closely related fish. Walleyes like large streams and lakes, prefer water temperatures below eighty-five, and feed heavily on other fish. They are often introduced as a predator species to reduce trash fish populations.

Walleyes spawn in spring right after the thaw in water of forty-five to fifty degrees. Although often caught in the daytime, walleyes are heavy nocturnal feeders. They seldom feed close to the surface, and they also tend to feed slowly and carefully, so lures and baits have to be presented just right to satisfy them. Crank baits and wobbling lures can go from doing nothing at all to catching walleyes like crazy with nothing other than a change of retrieve speed. Working a deep lure too rapidly is a common angler error in walleye fishing.

Walleyes are school fish, so that where you catch one, others should be available.

WHITE BASS (*Morone chrysops*)

This cousin of the striped bass has taken on added importance in recent years, since it has been crossed with that fish to create the hybrid striper. But the white bass has its own strengths, particularly a tendency to whallop lures and baits so hard that the angler thinks lightning has struck.

White bass are found mainly in the central states, and they like to spend most of the year in lakes and impoundments. They will migrate up streams and rivers that connect to the lakes in the spring and can often be caught in large numbers when they congregate below dams and other obstructions.

Shad are a favorite food, and white bass often herd schools of these bait fish to the surface in wild feeding sprees. At such times, big streamer flies and minnow-type lures will work well. When whites are deep, spinners and deep-running minnow lures score well, as do several live baits, particularly the shad that the whites feed on so avidly.

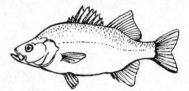

WHITE PERCH (*Morone americana*)

This is a versatile fish in terms of environmental tolerance; they are found in salt water and fresh water as well as in the brackish water in between. A relative of the striped bass, white perch are not nearly as large. The average fish weighs a pound or so, and a two-pounder is something to get excited about.

White perch are prolific, often too much for their own good. They can overpopulate an area and then become stunted from a lack of food. Whites are school fish, and fishing is largely a process of locating a concentration of them. Once you find them, the fishing is usually easy—whites eat anything and everything. Live bait, spinners, and flies all score well. Whites will even rise to dry flies during insect hatches.

During the spring spawning season, white perch migrate up freshwater streams, and this is the peak fishing season in most areas where the perch are found. Again, finding the moving schools is the key. If you can hit the concentrations right, you can catch a barrelful of white perch during the spawning run. In most states, limits are generous or even nonexistent for these prolific fish, and they are delectable on the plate.

YELLOW PERCH (*Perca flavescens*)

Although the name suggests it, the yellow and white perches are not related and do not even resemble each other to any degree. The yellow perch has an olive back, yellow sides, and a white belly. While not highly regarded as a sport fish, it is a good eating fish and is popular with anglers for that reason.

The yellow perch was originally an Eastern and Midwestern fish, but it has been widely planted elsewhere, particularly in lakes. Yellow perch are prolific, and overpopulation is often a problem in areas where natural predation is insufficient. Even in balanced environments, the yellow perch is a small fish; most weigh only a pound or so.

Yellow perch are usually easy to catch. They have undiscriminating appetites and will bite on whatever they are offered most of the time. Since they are school fish and easy to catch, they are ideal fish for young anglers just getting started. Offer them live bait, small spinners, or spinner-fly combinations. Unlike most other species, yellow perch often bite best during the brightest part of the day.

. . .

Be sure to keep in mind that nothing is certain about fishing except uncertainty. The information you acquire about fish, however you acquire it, should always be tempered by your willingness to experiment when standard methods don't work. There is always a time to throw the book away.

10

Hooking, Playing, and Landing Fish

By now you know about the kinds of tackle available and the conditions under which each is likely to be most beneficial, and you're also aware of the techniques and skills involved in selecting a bait or lure for a particular situation and presenting it through proper casting. Now we're ready to look ahead in time (and make the angler's "leap of faith") to the day when you hook, play, and land your first fish.

That's a day you won't soon forget, especially if the fish is a good-sized one that you've worked hard to locate and deceive into taking your bait or lure. For all too many beginning anglers, though, the first fish hooked is also the first "one that got away." That's because bringing a fish to net or hand involves more than just hooking it and reeling it in. That "more" is the subject of this chapter—we'll describe what you have to know and do to hook, play, and land a good fish successfully.

The Drag: Your Mechanical Advantage

Let's begin by describing the proper use of one of the most important and yet misunderstood weapons in the angler's arsenal: the *reel drag*. The drag is actually a reel brake that can be set at various levels of tension, thereby controlling the rate at which line can be pulled off the reel. A properly adjusted drag allows the reel spool to turn, yielding line, rather than allowing the strain to break the line. And by yielding the line only under pressure, the drag helps to tire the fish and restrict the distance and direction of its movements.

Many fishermen, even experienced ones, think that the function of the drag is to keep a fish from taking line off the reel. Not so. The true function of the drag is *to allow the fish to take line under conditions that favor the angler.* That's why the drag is there in the first place. If the idea were to stop the fish from taking line, there'd be no need for a drag; we'd simply design all reels so that the spool wouldn't turn in reverse. With such a setup, any fish strong enough to generate a force greater than the breaking strength of a given line would break off and escape, and any not so strong would be quickly reeled in and captured. But such a system wouldn't be very effective, or much fun either.

As you know, we choose lines with varying breaking strengths by considering several factors, only one of which is the size of the fish we're likely to encounter. And the weight of a fish isn't the only factor that contributes to the total strain on a fishing line; the friction of the rod guides, the drag of the water, and the force of the current all come into play. It doesn't take a six-pound fish to break six-pound-test line.

The ideal setting for a given drag, then, is a setting well below the breaking strength of the line, but tight enough so that the fish will have to expend energy making the drag slip.

It's important that you know how a drag operates so that you can adjust the drag properly and, just as important, select a reel with a good drag in the first place. Most of the drags on spinning, spin-casting, and bait-casting reels work by means of a spring that exerts pressure on a series of alternating hard and soft washers. As the drag adjustment is tightened, the spring exerts more pressure, compressing the soft washers between the hard ones allowing less slippage of the whole assembly and effectively braking spool rotation. Most spinning reel drags are adjusted by turning a nut in front of the spool, while spin-casting and bait-casting reels usually have a "star" drag adjustment on the handle shaft. Figure 10–1 will provide you with an illustration of the parts of a typical reel drag.

Fly reels have a drag, too, although they are different from those found on other types of equipment. The typical freshwater single-action fly reel has a ratchet-and-pawl arrangement, sometimes adjustable, which acts primarily to control spool overrun. Many fly anglers do not play most of their fish from the reel, but simply retrieve line with the line hand. When a fish big enough to take line from the reel is encountered, the reel drag is usually not sufficient, so the experienced angler provides additional resistance by pressing a finger on the revolving line or "palming" the exposed rim of the reel spool if such a rim is provided. Auto-

FIGURE 10–1 Exploded view of a typical drag system on a spinning reel

matic fly reels do have a drag similar to those on other reels, and this drag is adjustable on some models.

Although the alternating washer and spring arrangement is fairly simple, the quality of reel drags varies with the number and quality of the washers, the precision of the adjustment settings, and so forth. Although the more expensive reels usually have good drags, it is worthwhile to evaluate before you buy. A good drag is smooth; it engages without jerking and operates without chattering. Master angler Lefty Kreh has suggested a test that you can apply in the store (with the clerk's permission) to evaluate the drag of a given reel. If the drag is a good one, it should be possible for you to adjust it so that as you hold the line, the reel drops slowly and smoothly toward the floor, like a slow-motion yo-yo. If it takes a shake or a jerk to engage the drag or if the reel chatters or drops erratically, look for another reel.

SETTING THE DRAG

Setting the drag to the degree of resistance you want is a simple process mechanically, but it is complicated by a number of factors. For one thing, you must not only play the fish, but you must set the hook properly, too, and if the drag is set too lightly, the hook may not penetrate before the drag slips. And the conditions you fish in play a part as well. If you're fishing from a boat in an area with a lot of stumps, stickups, and other snags, you're going to want a pretty firm drag setting (and relatively heavy line) to stop a fish from taking you into a trouble spot. If you're wading a small stream and fishing with tiny spinners and two-pound line, you'll need a much lighter setting, or the fish will break your line just by striking the lure.

Another thing to keep in mind is that the drag setting is not a constant value, but a variable one. The effective drag increases as line is taken off the spool, because the drag is working against a spool of decreasing size and weight. And the mechanical drag that you adjust is not the only resistance your tackle provides to the fish. The guides of your rod add considerable friction, and the higher you hold the rod in playing the fish, the greater the resistance. You can easily break your line by horsing the fish too much, even if the mechanical drag is set well below the breaking strength of your line.

I recommend that you set your drag in the following manner, at least at the start: Tie your line to some object near ground level (a car bumper is good) and back off from it thirty feet or so, whatever you think represents a reasonable fishing distance in your circumstances. Now adjust the drag so that, as you raise the rod tip toward the vertical, the drag slips at about eleven o'clock on our imaginary clock face. Once you have this setting, pull the rod up hard as if you were setting the hook in a fish; the drag should slip at the same point, or close to it, each time whether you lift the rod sharply or easily. By using this method, you have taken into account the friction of the rod guides, and you have a setting tight enough to allow positive setting of the hook and rapid landing of small fish, but light enough to allow the good fish to take line *under conditions that favor you.*

Eventually you'll develop a "feel" for the proper drag setting and will be able to set it by just pulling some line off the reel and judging the resistance. But adjust it by the more complicated method first until you get the required experience. You'll need to adjust the drag each time you fish, not only because conditions change, but because *the drag should always be loosened after each day's fishing.* If you keep the drag tight for a prolonged period, the soft washers gradually lose their elasticity from being compressed, and the drag will become jerky or not slip at all. Many fishermen, even experienced ones, neglect to loosen the drag on their reels, so they're in a pretty precarious position when a good fish hits. Loosening the drag is a very important part of good reel maintenance.

Anglers who use bait-casting or spinning equipment have the same capability as the fly angler; because they have access to the reel spool, they can add drag with their fingers. If you fish with this equipment, you might want to adjust your drag a little more loosely than recommended, because you can always add more resistance with your thumb or finger. Using your fingers in this way is particularly crucial to ultralight fishing, because in this fishing the drag must be set very light to avoid breaking the frail line. Once the fish is hooked, you have much better control, because finger pressure is instantly adjustable and much more sensitive than a mechanical drag can be.

Don't underestimate how important a good drag and the proper drag setting can be in winning the struggle with a fish. A dramatic example of a drag's effectiveness was shown in a contest a few years ago between an expert angler and a champion swimmer. The line was attached to a lightweight harness around the swimmer's shoulders to approximate the angle and direction of line pull in an actual fishing situation. The rules were simple: the swimmer could swim as hard and in any direction as he wished, but could not attempt to break the line by any other method. The angler was to play the swimmer just as he would a fish, giving line when necessary and employing the reel drag as skillfully as he could.

The results were clear. The one-hundred-eighty-pound swimmer was rapidly played to exhaustion by an ordinary freshwater spinning outfit. And the line? Twelve-pound test!

Hooking the Fish

The situations an angler can face in trying to hook fish can cover a wide range from the "eye-crossing" strike of the bass angler driving the barb home through a tough plastic worm to the subtle lift of the fly angler "drawing" a tiny #28 midge hook into the corner of a brown trout's jaw.

All hooking situations have one thing in common: the sharper the hook, the more successful the hooking percentage of the angler. You should sharpen hooks as a matter of course, even brand new ones, and continue sharpening during the course of your fishing day, especially if you're fishing lures or baits that bounce along the bottom or have to be pulled from snags occasionally. There are many different hook hones available, including a new one that's battery powered, but they all have to be used to be effective. If your hooks are really sharp, fish will often hook themselves when they take the bait or lure.

Your hooking techniques have to be based on your tackle, your line, and the physical characteristics of the fish you're after. The solid strike you'd deliver to a northern pike would tear right through the mouth of a crappie, and the light strike that will pull a tiny hook securely home on four-pound line won't do a thing with a 1/0 hook and fifteen-pound line. And remember that the drag setting has to be complimentary to all of these variables.

Playing the Fish

It's no accident that we call the struggle after the fish takes the bait "playing the fish." A string with a fish on one end and a person on the other defines a situation of high enjoyment, at least for the person. Generally speaking, the object in playing the fish is to land it, and the pleasure of the struggle, a secondary consideration. On the other hand, the memories years later will not focus on the landing of the fish, or the killing of it, or even the eating, but the contest between fish and angler.

How you play a fish depends on your tackle, your temperament, and your situation. If you're fishing in a bass tournament, the object is to get the fish into the boat as fast as possible and into the live well so that the lure can get back into the water again. But when you're fishing just for fun, you'll probably want to savor those moments of connection with the fish.

In open water, you can let the fish run as it will, allowing the drag to tire the fish until you reel it in. If obstacles interfere, you'll try to snub the fish quickly to keep it out of trouble. If you're fishing in current, a fish that runs upstream is to your advantage, since it will tire much more quickly. So get below the fish if at all possible. If the fish runs downstream and has the power to keep going against your tackle, then you must follow as best you can and hope the fish will wear out before you do.

In all of these situations, the angle of your rod and your tactics in gaining line from the fish are important. Under most conditions, it is better to hold the rod at an angle to the water rather than directly vertical. It's true that a lot of photographs and paintings show the angler with the rod pointed at the heavens, but while that's a glamorous position, it's not a very efficient one. Fish, after all, are flexible from side to side but not from head to tail dorsally, so the fish finds it relatively easy to resist pressure from what to us would be an "over the shoulder" direction, but much more difficult to resist force applied from one side or another. So you can use a given rod angle not only to tire the fish faster, but also to influence its direction.

When you need to gain line, be sure to use the pumping technique discussed earlier. You do this by "lifting" the fish toward you with the rod and winding up the line you gained as the rod is dropped for another lift. If you've ever seen a film of a deep-sea angler fighting a big fish from a fighting chair, you've seen a graphic example of this technique. In freshwater fishing, the technique is exactly the same, though usually on a less strenuous scale.

Whatever you do, don't wind the reel handle against strong resistance, especially when using spinning and spin-casting tackle. The resulting line twist will either break your line right then and there or foul the line making later casting difficult.

Landing the Fish

For most anglers, the goal of playing the fish is to land it. Beginning anglers almost always try to land the fish too quickly when it is still full of fight ("green" in angler jargon) and quite able to put up strong resistance. Keep in mind that as you reel the fish in close to you, you are continually reducing the angle between your rod tip and the fish, and thereby greatly reducing the ability of the rod to absorb a sudden lunge. Remember, too, that a fish even partly out of water weighs a lot more than a fully immersed one, so it is able to put more strain on your equipment right at the end of the battle than at the beginning.

On the other hand, you should consider that playing the fish is stressful to it. If you know that the fish is too small to be kept, or if you plan to release it for any other reason, then try to land it quickly. If the fish escapes in the course of being landed while still strong, nothing is lost and the fish may have been saved.

TO NET OR NOT

Most anglers who want to keep the fish they hook use a landing net at least some of the time. Many others keep a net handy for landing the big or unusually stubborn fish even though they use it only rarely. A wading angler uses the short-handled type with a bag of moderate depth, but the boating fisherman needs a long-handled net with a deep bag. In either case, the trick in landing the fish with the net is to get the net into the water, then lead the fish over it, then lift. It's best to bring the fish into the net head first, so a last-minute burst of energy will drive the fish into the net rather than out of it. Beginners tend to wait until the fish is close to ready the net, then swipe at the fish with it, either breaking their line in the process or so terrifying the fish that it breaks the line with a final lunge for freedom.

Catch-and-release anglers often use a net even though they intend to release the fish, because they find it easier to handle fish in the net than with their bare hand. This is particularly desirable in handling trout and similar fish, because they are streamlined and slippery, difficult to get a good hold on. Whether you use a net or not, fish that are to be released should be handled as carefully and quickly as possible.

Some species of fish can be handled without the net by using other landing aids. Large fish may be gaffed, especially if they have sharp teeth or are otherwise dangerous. The basses can be immobilized by grasping their lower jaws between thumb and forefinger; this "lip-landing" technique is widely used, although it has the disadvantage of requiring that the fish be very close to the angler before being securely landed. Fish with sharp teeth and gill covers, like the muskellunge and pike, may be handled with "jaw spreaders," which hold their mouths open while lures are removed, and many catfish anglers like to hold these fish by special "pliers" that grip the lower jaw. You probably won't need such specialized gear to get started, but a landing net would be a good investment.

Fish for the Pan

If you're going to keep some fish for eating, two things ought to be considered: humaneness to the fish and protection of the fish's flavor until cooking. If you know for certain that you want to keep a particular fish, clean it quickly and put it on ice immediately (check Figure 10–2 for a good illustration of filleting procedure). If you're wading and can't carry an ice chest, one of the creels that cool by water evaporation will be suitable.

If you are keeping the fish only temporarily, for a tournament, for example, a live well is the answer. Many boats come with built-in live wells, and separate ones can be purchased or made. If the fish are to be kept for any length of time, an aerator is essential. Many boats come with these as standard equipment, or you can buy an aerator that will run off the battery that provides starting power for the motor.

Many anglers think that fish taste best if kept alive right up to the time of preparation for cooking. A live well is perfect for this, if you really can cook the fish rapidly after cleaning them, as you might be able to on a camping trip. But if you have to trailer your boat a considerable distance

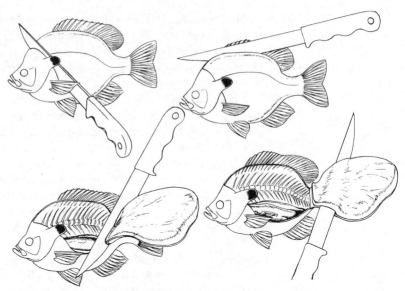

FIGURE 10–2 The steps involved in filleting a fish. Begin the sequence in the upper left, follow steps in clockwise order. Note that the filleting procedure eliminates the need for scaling and gutting the fish.

after the day's fishing, it's probably better to clean them promptly and get them on ice.

Releasing Fish

As I've indicated, you will release some of the fish that you catch, if only because they don't meet legal size or season requirements. But maybe you'll release more. Perhaps you don't care for fish at the table, so you have no reason to keep them. Or maybe you like to fish in the challenging "catch-and-release" and "special regulation" areas that are growing so popular around the country. If you become a serious trout fisherman or a tournament bass angler, you will probably release a majority of the fish that you catch.

If a fish is to be released at all, it should be released in good condition with a good chance of survival. This means first playing the fish efficiently, which may in turn mean foregoing the use of the lightest lines, especially during hot weather when water temperatures are high and oxygen content low. And the fish should be handled as little as possible, perhaps with a landing net. Never squeeze a fish that you intend to release, and don't put your fingers in the gills.

Barbless hooks are advantageous for releasing fish, because they usually do less damage and because they are much easier to remove quickly. When using barbless hooks, it is often possible to release a fish without touching it at all; you simply grasp the fly or lure and twist it out of the fish's mouth. Contrary to what many fishermen believe, barbless hooks are not less effective in hooking fish in the first place; they're more effective. Nor do many fish escape from barbless hooks before being landed. Many special regulation areas require barbless hooks. You can buy barbless hooks for fly tying, but most anglers just bend the barbs down on standard hooks, using needle-nose pliers.

Another thing you should consider if you're going to release a lot of your fish is using single hooks in place of the treble hooks that are standard on many lures. It's fairly easy to replace treble hooks with singles, and it may actually improve the performance of the lure, since single hooks penetrate more reliably than trebles and seem to hold just as well. Singles are not only easier to remove; they also eliminate much of the damage that treble hooks do. It's common for a fish to strike a lure with multiple treble hooks and get one set of trebles in the mouth, while another swings around and hooks a gill cover or an eye.

Finally, there will be times when a fish you want to release will be too exhausted to make it on its own, regardless of how carefully you tried to play and land it. This is especially likely in hot weather when lactic acid buildup in the fish's muscles is rapid. If a fish in this condition is to survive when released, you must provide artificial resuscitation. Fortunately, this does not have to be mouth-to-mouth resuscitation!

To relieve an exhausted fish, you must establish a flow of water over the gills. In current, you can do this by simply holding the fish with its head upstream. If the current is too slow, or if you're in a currentless area, you can push the fish away from you, draw it back, and push it away again. Since the fish is exhausted, you will not have to hold it tightly; with one hand, support the belly while gripping the tail with the other. Put the rod down and be prepared to work for a while on a played-out fish. It often takes several minutes to revive a fish, and fish practically always recover if you invest the necessary time.

Don't worry about when to release the fish. It will want to get away, and when it's strong enough, you won't be able to hold it, and it will swim from your hands and escape. And, considering that you came to catch it in the first place, you may be surprised at how good its escape makes you feel.

Like some of the other things we've covered, the skills involved in hooking, playing, and landing (and releasing) fish sound more complicated on paper than they really are in practice. Much that seems new now will seem obvious once you're on the water and will come to you pretty naturally. But it will come a lot more naturally if you've kept your hooks sharp, checked your line frequently, and adjusted your drag properly. When these things become habits, most of the fish you hook, you'll land.

CHAPTER **11**

Fishing Flowing Water

A recent fishing book contained the observation that when the water moves, the fish don't, and when the water doesn't move, the fish do. Like most generalizations about fishing, that one should be taken with a grain of salt; still, there are good reasons why fish that live in flowing water tend to move less than those in still water.

For one thing, swimming upstream in current requires a lot of effort, so it is not energy-efficient behavior. About the only time that fish swim upstream for appreciable distances is during spawning migrations when the reproduction urge overpowers more prudent considerations. Swimming downstream is easier, of course, but yet not so easy as you might think. For one thing, a fish swimming downstream must swim faster than the current in order to keep a flow of water moving over its gills; for another, a fish in really strong current has less directional control when swimming downstream. So distant, downstream migrations are not the result of individual decisions, but are part of the maturation process in particular species, particularly in the case of anadromous fish.

The most important thing to keep in mind is that flowing water carries food along with it. A stream fish has little need to move around in order to eat. A fish in current is presented with an endlessly moving cafeteria; all it has to do is sample as the banquet passes by.

So in water with current, fish tend to take up certain locations and remain in those locations for different purposes; for example, one location for feeding, another for resting. But these different locations are likely to be all in the same general area, and the fish is likely to remain in one of them for some time, unless disturbed.

Reading the Water

One of the most important skills the stream angler must develop is the ability to "read the water." This is the knack of knowing where the fish should be under particular circumstances. There are several different types of fish "lies."

THE FEEDING LIE (OR "FEEDING STATION")

Most important of these locations from the angler's standpoint is the feeding station, which is the position in the stream the fish assumes when it is feeding. In streams, feeding lies usually have two characteristics: current relief and access to food moving by in the stream's flow.

The fish needs current relief, because it would otherwise have to swim vigorously just to maintain its position in the stream. Such swimming would exhaust it eventually or at least burn up more energy than the fish was gaining by feeding—a poor metabolic bargain, indeed. So the fish takes up a position where some stream feature blocks or reduces the current for it while staying close enough to move into the current to intercept any morsels that might drift by. In addition to selecting a less stressful location, the fish also faces into the current, presenting the smallest possible surface area for the current to push upon while maintaining a good water flow over the gills and visual contact with the movable feast being carried downstream. This means that in most parts of the stream the fish will be facing upstream.

Learn to look for current lines that seem to offer some of the following advantages:

- *Rocks* break up the flow of the current and may harbor fish behind them, to the front, and along the sides.
- *Depressions* in the bottom may offer good current relief, while providing easy access to drifting food.

- *Conflicting currents* often cancel each other out and provide a haven of quiet water for a fish along with a large volume of food.
- *Stream curves* provide current relief in that the main flow usually presses against the outside of the curve, providing less stressful currents along the inside of the curve.

A good trick to speed your learning to read the water is to mark current lines by watching floating debris such as bits of foam, leaves, or small pieces of wood or bark. As you follow this flotsam, look for places with current differentials, that is, areas where swifter currents border on slower ones. These transitional areas offer good clues to the locations of feeding fish.

THE PROTECTIVE LIE

These lies are selected because they offer good protection from predators, especially overhead predators like ospreys and kingfishers. Deep water can provide protection, but keep in mind the concept of "cover" that we've mentioned so often in this book. A fish will be in or near an area where it can be safe.

In streams, undercut banks are favorite protective lies. Banks are most often undercut on the outside of stream curves where the current carves at the soil and rock. Rocks also provide cover, as do downed trees, weeds, and other stream features. Whenever one location can provide both protection and feeding opportunities, you have a prime lie where fish can be found most of the time. Learn to recognize such areas, and you'll catch a lot of fish.

THE RESTING LIE

Although fish do not sleep in the same way we do, they do require rest. The lies selected for resting have good protection and substantial current relief, although they usually do not present good feeding opportunities.

With knowledge of where fish are most likely to be found, you should make good progress in your stream fishing. In many cases, particularly when fishing small streams, you will be able to see the fish if you approach them carefully. Spend some time studying the locations they choose, and note these locations in a small notebook. Unless the stream changes drastically, fish will still be found in these locations years later.

In fishing larger rivers, you will not usually see the fish themselves, but you will catch some, and you will see fish feeding on the surface. A notation of these locations, along with the date, time of day, and pertinent information like weather conditions, water temperature, and water conditions, can provide you with information that will prove very useful in the future.

Finally, keep in mind that the lies of the fish change with stream conditions. A lie that is perfect for feeding during high water may be high and dry in late summer, and a weed bed that splits the current in low water will not do so when the stream is high. Keep in mind that fish do not choose lies on an idiosyncratic basis, but because these locations have certain biologically useful characteristics. Water you have learned to know is like a familiar book. It's still enjoyable to explore, and it will always contain a few surprises, but it is comfortable territory where you feel at home. And the fish will still be taking up the same stations generations from now.

. . .

The general methods that can be employed in fishing flowing waters can be reduced to three: still fishing, fishing from moving boats, and wading.

Still Fishing

Still fishing is usually identified with bank fishing, although it can be done from anchored boats as well. As the name implies, the angler is

FIGURE 11–1 An illustration of some typical stream features that provide cover and current relief for fish. Fish will select those areas that provide protection, relief from stress, and feeding opportunities.

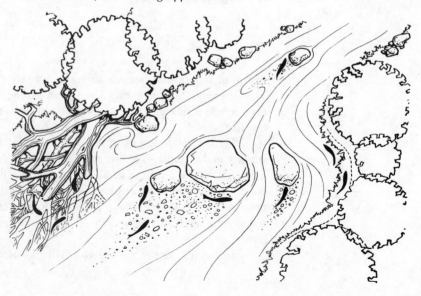

stationary in the process although movement from one point to another is common.

Still fishing is usually bait fishing, and it is most often practiced for bottom-feeding fish like carp and catfish. Two main techniques may be employed, and how they work will depend on whether the angler is working from a boat or from shore. With the bobber method, the bait is suspended from a bobber, which is used both to signal the strike and to suspend the bait at what the angler thinks will be a productive level. If the bobber method is used from an anchored boat, the bobber and bait are allowed to float downstream from the boat to any distance desired. If the boat is allowed to drift, the bobber drifts along with it at a distance determined by the length of the cast. When the bobber method is used in bank fishing, the bobber and bait will usually have to be recast repeatedly as they drift through the chosen fishing area.

If a bobber is not used, it is possible to anchor the line on the bottom with an appropriate sinker, as discussed in Chapter 2. With this method, the bank fisherman can hold the bait in a particular area for a prolonged period, or if a slightly undersized sinker is chosen, the bait can be cast upstream and allowed to bounce along the bottom until another cast is necessary.

Still fishing is relaxing fishing. It is particularly well suited to hot summer nights and cold beer.

Fishing from Boats

In flowing water, a boat can be used as an anchored platform for still fishing or as a floating platform for casting either bait or lures. A variation on these themes is the "float," in which the boat is used both as a moving casting platform and as transportation from one good wading or still fishing spot to another. No one boat can do all of these things perfectly, so many anglers use more than one type of craft or choose a single boat that is a compromise, able to fulfill a number of functions moderately well. Here are some of the possibilities.

THE RIVER BOAT

Preferences vary in different parts of the country, but the typical river boat is usually a shallow-draft boat of ten to sixteen feet, often powered by a small outboard motor. A particular favorite is the flat-bottom, or "johnboat." Many johnboats are still built by local craftsmen of wood, but they are also offered in aluminum and fiberglass by commercial boat builders. The johnboat is especially stable, so it makes a good platform for comfortable still fishing and can be used for drift casting, too, where conditions do not require great maneuverability. Because of their shallow water capability, johnboats are especially popular in many Eastern rivers. But the classic flat-bottom johnboat sacrifices maneuverability, so that anglers who want to use a boat for drifting and casting often prefer a modified or combination hull design in which rounded contours and an upswept bow contribute to ease of maneuver.

Speed is an important consideration for some river boat owners. The flat-bottomed boat is a slow craft compared to boats with V-shaped hulls. A compromise chosen by many anglers is the "semi-V," which combines some of the stability of the flat-bottomed hull with the planing efficiency of the contoured hull.

Today's river boats are usually fitted with a number of accessories. *Anchors* are usually of the "mushroom" variety and rubber-coated; such anchors are quiet and don't get caught in bottom obstructions as often as the sharp-angled types. Ten-to-fifteen-pound anchors are sufficient for most river boats. Another way to hold a boat still is the "brush anchor." Attached to tree limbs on islands or those that overhang shorelines, the brush anchor has the advantage of not pulling down on the upstream side of the boat, as conventional anchors do, which makes brush anchors especially good for still fishing during high or rising water, as you might wish to do if you favor catfish. And in areas where the water can rise rapidly, such as downstream from dams which release water, brush anchors have a decided safety advantage, since they allow the boat to rise with the water, at least up to the level where the anchors are attached. Nevertheless, anchor ropes should always be fabric, and the prudent angler always keeps a sharp knife handy. Anglers have been drowned when an anchor caught in strong current or when the river rose suddenly with an anchor wedged between rocks on the bottom. If the anchor cannot be cut loose in such a situation, it may pull the boat under as the water rises.

A recent innovation that avoids a lot of trouble is the *remote-*

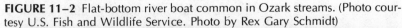

FIGURE 11–2 Flat-bottom river boat common in Ozark streams. (Photo courtesy U.S. Fish and Wildlife Service. Photo by Rex Gary Schmidt)

controlled anchor system, which allows the boat operator to lower or raise anchors without leaving his seat. This not only adds convenience, but it also cuts down on noise. When the angler has to move from one end of the boat to the other to raise or lower anchors, noise is practically inevitable.

Another way to defeat noise is to install *carpeting* on the deck of the boat. This is so popular now that many boats come with carpet already installed. Carpeting not only reduces noise, but makes the boat safer by providing more secure footing. And, when small items of tackle are dropped, they stay where they fall on a carpeted surface; on an uncarpeted deck, they invariably roll under a seat or disappear underneath a support rib.

Many river boat users like the convenience of an *electric trolling motor*. These motors are extremely quiet, and they make it possible to maneuver the boat silently along a shoreline while the angler casts or to hold the boat stationary in current. Some trolling motors can be controlled by the operator's foot, others by hand. Some boat anglers have one of each type for use in different circumstances.

Although they are not as widely used in river boats as in those used for lake and impoundment fishing, *depth-finding sonar* units may be helpful. These devices provide information about depth and can also show a picture of the bottom contour. Under the right conditions, a

FIGURE 11–3 Lowrance 2260, a popularly priced sonar unit (Courtesy Lowrance Electronics, Inc.)

skilled user can spot schools of fish or even large individual fish. The most sophisticated of these units can print a picture of the structure on graph paper, making available a permanent record of the bottom features of a particular section of river.

Motors for river boats are usually of small displacement and run on a mixture of oil and gasoline, although four-cycle engines that run on gasoline alone are becoming more popular. Since most river boats operate in shallow water some of the time, protection for the vulnerable propeller is a must. Most popular is a *fork* arrangement, which attaches to the shaft in front of the propeller and shields the prop from rocks. Some anglers make their forks by modifying pitchforks, while others fabricate strong forks from scratch using steel rod. Since the fork reduces top speed, many anglers prefer a fork that can be removed when boating in deep water.

In addition to protection for the propeller, anglers who often use their boats in shallow water usually want the added protection of *shallow-water drive*. This feature allows the motor to tilt up when an obstruction is hit or to be tilted manually by the operator. Motors designed for shallow-water operation must have the water pump intake located so that the motor can be operated in the tilted position without overheating. Many of the most popular small-displacement motors come with shallow-water drive as standard equipment; on some others, it is available as an option.

THE DRIFT BOAT

Some boats are designed specifically for drift fishing in which the angler casts repeatedly while the boat keeps moving. One advantage of drift fishing is that it allows a natural presentation of bait, lure, or fly, since the boat and the bait are drifting at the same speed as the current. Another major advantage of drift fishing is that a lot of river can be covered in a day's fishing; it is typical to cover several miles of river in a drift.

Swift rivers, of which there are many in the American West, are often fished by the drift method, and special boats are used to take advantage of the special conditions that typify these rivers. Inflatable rafts are popular on very swift rivers. When equipped for fishing (rather than the white water excursions for which they are also used), these rafts utilize special seats and a rowing frame made of steel or aluminum tubing. The boat operator (who is usually the fishing guide) controls the boat with oars while the angler casts. In the hands of a skilled operator, the inflatable raft is a safe, comfortable, and highly maneuverable fishing platform.

Specially designed boats made of wood or fiberglass are also widely used for drift fishing swift rivers. These boats are usually asymmetrical in design with a long, pointed bow. Like the raft, the drift boat is controlled by oars manned by an expert, usually a guide. The sleek shape makes it possible for a skilled oarsman to hold the boat in position for a time or even row it upstream for short distances in foaming fast water. Typically, the angler stands or sits in the bow while the guide mans the oars. On larger boats, two anglers can be accommodated.

THE CANOE

Canoes are highly desirable fishing boats when used in shallow rivers of moderate current. The canoe is a lightweight, easy to handle, and highly maneuverable craft, and it can carry quite a lot of gear if packed properly. Canoes are not as stable as boats, and thus they do not lend themselves to vigorous casting, but experienced canoeists can cast well from canoes as long as they keep a low center of gravity (preferably kneeling on the canoe bottom) and they content themselves with casts of modest distances. Since the canoe is capable of very quiet operation, the careful angler doesn't need such long casts anyway.

Most anglers experienced with float trips think that the best float is one that combines about half wading with half drifting. For this sort of float, the canoe is the perfect craft. When you spot an area that you want to fish carefully, the canoe allows a quiet approach and is easily landed and secured while you fish. Setting off again is as easy as getting in the canoe and shoving off.

Aluminum canoes are still the most popular with anglers, but the newer plastic and fiberglass models are growing in favor. Aluminum is durable and relatively lightweight, but it dents easily, and it is hard to be

FIGURE 11–4 The canoe is an ideal craft for floating and fishing quiet rivers. (Photo courtesy The Coleman Company)

FIGURE 11–5 Many canoes can handle a small outboard motor. (Photo courtesy U.S. Fish and Wildlife Service. Photo by Dr. F. Eugene Hester)

quiet in an aluminum canoe, especially when negotiating riffles. Plastic or fiberglass canoes are quiet, and, since they flex slightly when hitting an obstacle, they can slide over a rock or ledge on which an aluminum canoe might get hung up. Plastic canoes require little maintenance, since the color is impregnated in the body material of the canoe. The glass or plastic canoes don't dent, although they can be punctured if a sharp rock is hit at high speed.

It is possible to supplement paddle-power with a small motor when using a canoe. Some canoes are made with square sterns to accommodate motors, while the standard canoes can utilize a special side-mounting bracket to hold the motor. Gasoline motors in the one-to-five horsepower range are the most common, but electric trolling motors are gaining in popularity. A trolling motor with enough thrust to maneuver a big bass boat will push a canoe along smartly.

Whatever craft you end up using for your fishing, be sure to learn and follow the rules of boating safety. A boating course is probably available to you; if not, at least get some of the literature on safety available from the Coast Guard. And wear a flotation vest. Those pictured in Figure 11–6 are especially good, because they provide the convenience of a fishing vest with the safety of a personal flotation device.

Wading

If you fish small streams or if you like to take river float trips, much of your fishing time will be spent wading. Many anglers prefer to wade whenever possible; they feel that they fish better when actually sharing the water environment with the fish. And while the wading angler cannot move as rapidly as the boating fisherman, he has the advantage of

FIGURE 11–6 Two flotation fishing vests from Stearns. The vest on the right is inflatable. It can be blown up by mouth using a hidden valve, or, in an emergency, inflated instantly by pulling the tab above the lower left pocket. (Photo by the author)

being able to position himself much more precisely for approaching and casting to the fish. Finally, don't overlook the comfort of wading. On a hot summer day, wading in a bathing suit and sneakers can be a delightful way to cool off and be entertained at the same time.

Wading anglers usually follow the maxim that feeding fish face upstream, so they fish upstream in order to approach the fish from behind. Wading requires stalking skills in order to approach the fish without spooking them, and this is especially true when the light is bright and the water shallow. If you're going to be a serious wading angler, be careful to keep low, avoid casting your shadow over the fish, and don't wear bright clothing or accessories that flash reflected light.

In your wade fishing, you're likely to spend most of your time with a fly rod or spinning rod in hand. These two methods lend themselves to the delicate presentation of small lures and baits, and you'll need to use these tactics to arouse the interest of a good fish when conditions are tough and the fish most cautious.

Since you'll be fishing upstream most of the time, you'll be casting upstream, too. If you're using spinners, remember that they must be retrieved faster than the speed of the current or the blades won't turn. Keep in mind, too, that lures will sink more deeply on an upstream presentation than when cast across or downstream.

When using flies, either surface or wet, what you're trying to do is present the fish with a fly that looks and *behaves* like natural food. When the food you're representing is an insect, you must cast and control your fly line so that the fly floats or drifts as the natural insect would, without drag. Drag occurs when the current pulls or pushes on the line in such a way that the fly is pulled out of a natural line of drift and across the current. Since food freely floating in the water doesn't do this, drag is interpreted by fish as unnatural, and they avoid dragging flies most of the time. Trout are particularly noted for detecting drag and shunning the flies that exhibit it. You can learn to detect drag on your fly by using floating debris as an indicator; constantly compare the drift of your fly to anything in the stream that is floating freely. Learning to cast a slack line is one of the major tricks in defeating drag. However you manage it, remember that your goal is to give your fly that same kind of unattached freedom of movement.

As in any other specialized fishing technique, one of the secrets of successful wading is having the right equipment and accessories. Keeping yourself warm and dry while wading in cool weather is essential, and maintaining good footing on the bottom is crucial at any time.

WADERS AND WADING SHOES

The first question you face is, "Do I need waders?" If you fish mostly in the hot months, the answer is probably no. Even a cool trout stream is not too cold for July and August wading in most of the country, particularly since in small stream wading, you are in and out of the stream instead of being immersed for long periods. But if you fish larger water or during the cool months of the year, you need wading gear.

But what sort of waders do you need? Hip waders? Chest-highs? Felt sole or cleat sole? Stocking foot or boot foot? You must evaluate these questions according to the conditions you think you'll face. If you need to wade in waters of varying depths, then you need chest waders. If you're going to be wading only shallow streams where wading consists of putting a foot in here and there or maybe fording the stream occasionally, hip boots will do fine, and they have the advantage of being easier to get on and off, somewhat more comfortable (especially in hot weather), and cheaper than chest waders.

Both hip boots and waders are available in felt-sole and lug-sole versions. If you fish in upland freshwater streams, get the felt-soled type, because the streams you will fish are rocky and slippery. If you fish in tidal waters, the cheaper lug-soled boots will probably suffice, because most of your streams will have sand or soil bottoms.

Suppose that you decide that you need chest waders. Now you have an additional decision to make: Whether to buy the boot-foot type or the stocking-foot version, which require the addition of wading shoes. Again, this is a matter of personal preference. But you should know that anglers who wade a great deal prefer the stocking-foot type, because they find that the added support and security that comes with good wading shoes more than offsets the additional expense and inconvenience. Even if you do a lot of wet-wading, with no waders at all, you will find a good pair of wading shoes a good investment in your comfort and security. If you are an occasional wet-wader, an old pair of tennis shoes will suffice, especially if you take the time to glue some outdoor carpet to the soles. Figure 11–7 will give you an idea of some of the options available in wading shoes.

WADING STAFF

If you're going to wade swift waters, a wading staff will add to your safety. You can always cut one at streamside in a pinch, but finding the right size sapling and then cutting it always seems a problem when you need it. Commercial staffs are available in a couple of configurations: the folding type, which you can carry in your vest, will zip open when you pull it from its pouch, and the solid types, which are made from hard woods or aluminum. Or you can make your own—an old ski pole is a good starting point.

OTHER WADING AIDS

Sometimes you face conditions so treacherous that even felt soles don't provide enough security. For such times, you can resort to wading

FIGURE 11–7 Three approaches to the wading shoe. *Foreground:* traditional leather and felt-sole shoes from the Russell Moccasin Company. *Left:* Danner River Grippers, featuring synthetic felt soles and lightweight inserts. *Rear:* old tennis shoes with carpet glued to the soles. (Photo by Katherine Lee)

chains or sandals that provide the grip of metal bars when installed over your standard boots or wading shoes. You can also buy a mixture of grit and glue to apply to the soles of your shoes. I know one fellow who smears shoemaker's cement on the soles of his boots and then sprinkles them with metal shavings from the floor of his dad's sheetmetal shop.

In the final analysis, your biggest wading aid is your own prudence. Few fish are worth risking your life to get to, and drowning isn't

FIGURE 11–8 Specially designed wading jacket from Early Winters, Ltd. features Gore-Tex fabric, roomy outside pockets, and velcro-closed access panels for reaching vest contents on the inside. (Photo by Katherine Lee)

the only way you risk your life when wading in treacherous water. Hypothermia is always a danger when you get soaked, even in warm weather. Real wading skill can come only from experience, but here are a few tips.

1. Use a wading staff.
2. Stand sideways to the current. By doing so, you provide less surface for the river to push on.
3. When crossing a swift current, move slowly, advancing one foot at a time. Plant the upstream foot securely, then move the downstream foot over to meet it.
4. Never turn your back on the river. If you must stand square to the current, face it.
5. If you feel yourself losing your balance, thrust your rod into the water on the side toward which you are falling. It may provide enough leverage for you to regain your balance.
6. If the current takes you off your feet, try to remain upright, and keep your feet moving, searching for the bottom. If you keep calm, chances are the current will soon take you to shallower water where you can regain your footing.

There is disagreement among anglers over whether or not you should wear a belt around your chest waders as a safety aid. Some argue that the belt will keep your waders from filling with water; others insist that to have the top half of your waders full of water while the leg area is full of air reduces your stability. While my own personal view inclines to the second position, the best way to be sure that you can handle swamped waders is to intentionally swamp them and learn how it feels. Choose a quiet stretch of river or a swimming pool, and be sure someone is with you to help, if need be. Then fill your waders and swim around in them. You'll find that while full waders slow you down considerably, they will not pull you under and that you can negotiate. This experience will help to keep you from panicking when you step into a hole for the first time. And panic is a lot more dangerous than swamped waders.

FLOAT TUBES

It's hard to know just where to include the float tube. It's part wading, part float fishing. While the tube originated in lake and pond fishing, it has now found a place in river fishing, too.

The original float tube was just a big truck tire inner tube with a crude canvas seat across the hole. Today's tubes, though, have all the comforts of home. A modern tube will have a cover that completely encloses the tube, several zippered pockets and pouches to hold gear, an "apron" across the front to keep water out for the angler wearing waders, and even an extra tube in back to provide additional support for the angler's back. As in wading, the fisherman may tube "wet" or use chest waders in combination with the tube to stay dry.

The tube makes it possible for the wading angler or the person who doesn't want the cost or inconvenience of a boat to reach fish in deep water. When combined with swim flippers, the tube can provide fairly quick transportation into casting range of an enticing spot. And, properly used, float tubes are safe. The tough, nylon fabric that tube systems are made of protects the inner tube from hook puncture, and these tubes hold so much air that a slow leak allows time for an angler to make it to shore on most waters except, perhaps, the big impoundments. When you consider the fact that many float systems have two tubes, or chambered compartments, the margin of safety is obvious. The major danger associated with float tubing is angler carelessness or stupidity. A number of fishermen have been drowned or injured attempting to use tubes on swift, white water rivers. Float tubes are not designed for such conditions—they are for placid water, either lakes, ponds, or slow rivers.

The coming thing? Tube camping. Some hardy anglers are spending the night in their tubes, far out on big impoundments, adding anchors and umbrella hats to insure their comfort and safety. But you needn't go that far to see how the tube can add to your fishing success.

Obviously, we have only touched the surface of fishing flowing water. Each river and stream has its mysteries, and each has its resident sages who have devoted their leisure hours to discovering the answers to these mysteries. In that sense, this chapter is a lot like the surface of a flowing stream—it has provided a few clues, but the depths are for your own exploration.

12

Still Water Angling

Summer comes late to central Pennsylvania, but when it comes, the heat can be oppressive. At the end of humid summer days like this, my friend Dave Henrie and I would head for Raystown Lake for some relaxed catfishing. We'd each take a pair of rods with plenty of worms, shrimp, and liver for bait. Our cooler would be filled with beer, ham sandwiches, and various snacks, and a portable radio served to fill in the few spare moments between snatches of conversation.

Our fishing was not strenuous. We selected our shoreline spot with an eye for our own comfort more than anything else and baited up only when we were satisfied that we would be comfortable for a long stay. With a heavy sinker installed to hold the bait near the bottom, we attached two hooks to each line, one above the other, each baited with a different morsel. After casting, we propped the rods in forked sticks, opened the bails so that a fish picking up the bait would feel no resistance, and lightly tied a tissue around the line just where it left the last guide at the end of the rod. The tissue was our strike indicator; when it began to jiggle we would get up, stroll over to the rod and pick it up, and wait for the cattie to take line. When it did, we'd close the bail, set the hook, and reel in another catfish to toss in the cooler. There are certainly more exciting and exacting forms of still water angling, but few more satisfying, and those cool nights spent beside the waters of Raystown Lake linger pleasantly in my memory.

What we call still water angling is fishing in ponds, lakes, and impoundments. To call all these waters "still" is something of an overstatement, because they do move to some extent, both as the result of wind and wave action on the surface and because of the sinking and rising of water as it changes density with changes in temperature. But these waters do not have currents, and the behavior of the fish that inhabit them differs from that of stream fish. The angler who pursues these fish will have to adapt tackle and techniques to their activity.

A fish in still water is motivated by the same drives that control its brethren in flowing water: Survival first and foremost, with feeding and safety the primary components of this urge. The problem for the lake or pond fish is that there is no current to carry food to it. So the fish must move to find food, and, while doing so, it must remain alert for its own safety. In fishing still water, the most essential of the angler's skills is *finding the fish.* For now, keep one principle in mind: *In any body of still water, the great majority of the water contains no fish at all.* If you fish blind, you'll very likely conclude that "they aren't biting," when, in fact, you may not be fishing where the fish are.

Fishing Lakes and Impoundments

America is a land of lakes. The northern tier of states has always had an abundance of natural lakes, but in this century the South, Southwest, and Far West have become lake country, too, thanks to an extraordinary binge of dam-building. These dams impound the flow of rivers and produce huge man-made lakes. The reasons for dam-building are numerous; flood control, irrigation, power generation, and commercial development of lake shoreline are some of the most important. The enthusiasm of Congress for pork barrel water projects has played a major role, as has the fondness of the Army Corps of Engineers for dam-building. But, whatever the reason, the creation of these lakes has spurred a type of fishing that never existed before and has contributed to the rapid increase in the popularity of fishing across the country.

But some of these lakes are huge; they may have hundreds of miles of shoreline, numerous little inlets and bays, and miles of open water from shore to shore. How do you fish water like that? It has taken thirty years of experimentation to find out, but there are now thousands of anglers who know how to do it. They find fish by studying four critical variables: temperature, structure, cover, and depth.

TEMPERATURE

As you already know, water temperature is perhaps the most important factor influencing the behavior of fish. In still waters, temperature controls the *location* of fish, as well as their behavior, because the density of water changes with its temperature. In deep lakes, the water is stratified in layers of varying temperatures. In technical terms, this phenomenon is called *thermal stratification.*

Let's look at thermal stratification. Water is at its heaviest at a temperature of thirty-nine degrees Fahrenheit; at temperatures above or below this point, water becomes lighter and tends to rise. This phenomenon keeps lakes from freezing solid in cold weather—they freeze from the top down rather than from the bottom up! And it means that the lightest, and therefore the coldest, water lies right under the ice in winter, while water at lower depths is warmer. See Figure 12–1 for an illustration of winter stratification.

With the coming of spring, the surface ice melts and the water at the top of the lake rapidly warms to the temperature of the water in the depths. Now, breezes can mix all the waters in the lake, because all are of similar density. Oxygen and nutrients that may have been depleted at the bottom of the lake can now be replenished by this mixing action. This is the period of *spring overturn.*

With summer, a new stratification takes place. As the water in the upper layer becomes warm, the lake gradually stratifies into three

FIGURE 12–1 Thermal stratification

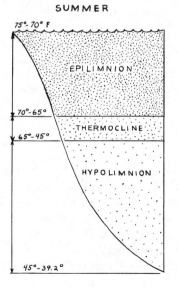

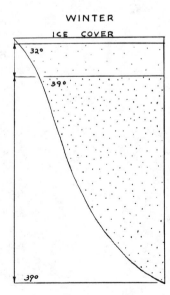

clearly defined layers. The upper layer, called the *epilimnion*, is influenced directly by air temperature. It is the warmest water in the lake and is constantly being mixed by wind and wave action. This upper layer lies atop a layer of rapidly declining temperature called the *thermocline*. The thermocline may be thought of as a transition zone between the warm water at the top of the lake and the cold water at the bottom. Keep in mind that because of the rapid temperature changes that are typical of the thermocline, locating fish in this area of the lake may depend on depth adjustments of just a few feet.

Below the thermocline is the *hypolimnion,* or cold-water zone. In lakes of sufficient depth, the temperature of most of this zone will be right around thirty-nine degrees, because such water is heaviest and sinks to the bottom. See Figure 12–1 for an illustration of summer stratification.

With the arrival of autumn, the lake overturns again. The water in the epilimnion is cooled and begins to sink. As the temperature of the waters in the upper layers approaches the temperature of the hypolimnion, the waters freely mix again, bringing oxygen and nutrients to the depths once more. With winter, falling temperatures start the cycle over again.

Lakes that do not freeze over in winter do not stratify, so the waters freely circulate at all levels, and the temperature is constant from top to bottom. Such a lake may be more inhospitable to fish than one that freezes, since the hypolimnion of a frozen lake (being about thirty-nine degrees) might be several degrees warmer than the waters of an unstratified lake.

This stratification process has important influences on the location of fish in still waters. Many cold water species will be unable to tolerate the high temperatures of the upper layer during summer. On the other hand, the deepest levels of a lake might not carry sufficient oxygen to support fish at various times of the year. And keep in mind that these temperatures and oxygen variations influence the location of forage fish, and game fish predators are never far away from these food sources.

STRUCTURE

Structure is the term anglers use to describe the physical features of the bottom of a lake. Structure is important to locating fish because the species that anglers seek most often prefer to hold close to particular types of underwater formations. Largemouth bass, for example, are partial to underwater ridges and bars; if you can locate an old creek bed, the remains of an old road bed, or the decaying stumps of trees that once marked a fence line, largemouth may very well be suspended close to or over them. Most areas that offer sudden dropoffs to deeper water hold good potential for harboring game fish.

COVER

As we've stressed from the beginning of this book, fish never stray too far from what they regard as an area where they can be safe from predators. What this cover is depends on the lake and its own special features, and it depends on the cover preferences of the fish being sought. Underwater cover includes geological formations or remnants of physical features of the land before being flooded, so cover and structure can often refer to the same underwater area. Overhead cover includes tops of flooded trees, lakeside weed beds, lily pads, deadfalls, and such. Sunken weed beds a few feet under the surface provide excellent cover at in-between depths.

DEPTH

The depth at which fish are found depends mainly on water temperature and the related variable of oxygen supply. Warm water cannot hold as much dissolved oxygen as cooler water, so fish often go deep during late summer to find more oxygen. Keep in mind, though, that depth interacts with structure and cover; just because you note a promising water temperature at a certain depth doesn't mean you've located the fish. Now you should look for that temperature at a similar depth in an area where you know that favorable structure and cover are available.

EQUIPMENT AND TECHNIQUES

Much of the remainder of this chapter will deal with equipment and techniques you can use to gather information about temperature, structure, cover, and depth. When faced with a new lake, however, you're in a position of not knowing the territory. Under these conditions, even experienced anglers need special aids. Here are some things you can do.

Hire a Guide. There's probably not a big lake in the country that doesn't have several guides working it, and it would be worth your while to invest in their services. If you have several days to fish a lake, going out with a guide the first day or two can save you an enormous amount of trial and error.

Guides are like any other group; there are good ones and not-so-good ones. The good ones teach you as you fish; they not only want you to catch fish, they want you to know why and how you're catching them. The good guides are looking for returning customers and word-of-mouth advertising, and they'll work hard to see that you're satisfied. Your part of the bargain is to follow the guide's advice and instructions to the letter, while letting him know the kind of fishing that you like and what you hope to learn more about. Be sure to ask questions, and don't be shy about taking notes if you doubt your ability to remember all that the guide has to say. You're paying for expertise, and you should derive all the benefit you can from it.

A couple of cautions: Make your plans well in advance so that you have time to investigate the reputations of several guides before making your choice. Be sure you know about local custom: Do you provide lunch or does the guide? Does the guide expect to be paid in advance or at the end of the day? How long does the guide expect to fish with you? Finally, be sure to match the guide's expertise with your fishing preferences. If you like to fish surface plugs, you won't enjoy an outing with a guide who specializes in probing deep structure with plastic worms or jigs.

Ask Questions. Find a marina or public boat launch area, and strike up conversations with anglers returning from a day on the water. Don't bother being subtle; tell them you're new to the area and are wondering if they've learned anything you might benefit from. You'll find most anglers willing to give you a tip or two, but be reasonable and don't press for too much detail. If a fellow says, "They're taking crankbaits at fifteen feet," that's a mighty generous piece of information. Don't expect him to go ahead and give you the exact location of his favorite "honey hole" and describe the lure and retrieve speed, too. You've got to be ready to take a tip and interpret it in light of what you already know. If he said fifteen feet, chances are he means fifteen feet over submerged structure rather than fifteen feet over eighty feet of open water. Now if you can find locations nearby that offer good structure at about that depth, you're ready to start experimenting on your own.

Get Maps of the Area. Most marinas and tackle shops will carry maps of the lake area. If the lake is new, even a road map might reveal under-water structure resulting from the inundation of old roads, creeks, and buildings. Topographic maps available from the U.S. Geological Survey will show the elevation and contours of the lake bottom as it was before being flooded.

The best maps for lake anglers are called hydrographic maps; they show contour in five- or ten-foot intervals, which is the kind of precision you need. You may need to write to the Fish and Game Department of the state involved. If the impoundment was a federal project, contact the U.S. Geological Survey, GSA Building, Washington, DC, 20242, and request hydrographic maps of the lake you're interested in. While you're writing, ask for an index of available lake maps that you can use in planning future trips. Be prepared to spend a few dollars for good maps.

Learn to Read the Shoreline. You can use shoreline features to help orient yourself to a map or to give you a rough idea of the bottom even when you don't have a map. The land under water is usually a continuation of the contour you can see. If a rocky bluff dips straight off into the water, the odds are good that the steep drop continues into deep water below. If a spit of land gradually descends into the lake, chances are that the gradual descent continues under water. In fact, any place where a sloping point continues into the water is a good place to start prospecting if you don't have more certain methods for locating fish. By casting along such a descending bar and using the countdown method of determining the depth of your lure, you can systematically probe deeper and deeper water until you get a strike, and then you can fish hard at the same depth.

Use a Depth Finder. Most serious lake anglers wouldn't think of going near the water without their sonar units. These devices use a transducer mounted in or under the boat to send inaudible sound waves toward the bottom. The waves hit solid objects and bounce back, are intercepted by the transducer, and are converted to light impulses, which show up on a

FIGURE 12–2 The Lowrance X-15 Grayline Recorder. This is one of the most advanced sonar units, featuring computerized functions, extreme depth capability, and permanent paper recording of bottom features. (Courtesy Lowrance Electronics, Inc.)

screen in the boat. Depth finders can give a clear picture of the lake bottom structure, as well as show the depth of the prominent bottom features. They can even pinpoint the locations of fish. And modern depth finders can read the lake bottom at high speed, up to seventy miles per hour. By using one as you cruise, you can spot promising fishing areas. If you go over the same route frequently, you will grow familiar with the bottom and be able to use the finder to go right back to a favorite spot.

Use a Depth Thermometer. You know the importance of water temperature, and you know that water stratifies in layers in lakes. If you know the temperature preferences of the game fish you're seeking, you can establish rather quickly how deep the fish should be. If you can find cover at that depth, the fish should be there, too. And if they are fish that require really cold water, such as lake trout, finding the proper depth alone will probably be sufficient.

The simplest thermometer is the same one you'd use for stream fishing, attached to a line marked in one-foot intervals. Locating the ideal temperature zone with such an outfit is time consuming since you must leave the thermometer suspended for a minute or so at each chosen depth to get a stable reading. Another problem is that when you have the thermometer down deep, the water temperature above may alter the reading as you pull the thermometer to the surface. The better system, if you can afford it, is the boat-mounted temperature probe and on-board readout unit. With this setup, you don't need to haul the thermometer up to read it, but will receive a readout on board the boat at each level where you pause in lowering the probe. Some of these devices can provide an almost instant readout, and most require no more than thirty seconds or so to stabilize at an accurate reading. If you plan to fish often for lake trout, walleyes, or other fish that spend a lot of time in very deep water, one of these units might be worth its weight in gold. If you're strictly a bass and panfish angler, the simple string-and-thermometer rig will work fine if you don't mind taking the time, because these fish are likely to be in relatively shallow water most of the time.

Try Trolling. Trolling is an excellent method of finding fish in unfamiliar water, because you're moving your lure through a lot of water area rather than sitting in one place. When you get a strike while trolling, you can stop and fish that location hard; chances are, there are more fish in that same area.

To troll effectively, you've got to think of trolling as a way of exploring layers of water as well as a large surface area. This means that you must have knowledge of your lures and how they work when being trolled. How deep will a given lure go, and how is the depth influenced by trolling speed? Is the action of a lure different when trolled than it is when the same lure is being retrieved after casting? You'll need to know about trolling sinkers, too. In short, you have to know where in the water your trolled lure is, so that when you get the strike you've waited for, you'll know how to fish out the location successfully.

Work the Shoreline. If you don't have the time to explore an unfamiliar lake, don't have sophisticated equipment, and can't afford to hire a guide, or if you're the type who just likes to keep it simple, then fish along the lake shoreline with surface and shallow running lures. Morning and evening will provide the best opportunities here, as bass and other predator fish move into shallow water to prey on minnows, crayfish, and such. Sloping shoreline provides the best bet most of the time, because it suggests a gradually sloping bottom along which you can manipulate your bait or lure. Be alert for rocky points and bars; anchor your boat at right angles to these locations, and you can fish them systematically from shallow to deeper water.

You're not likely to wow the folks back at the marina with the size and extent of your catch using these simple methods, but you're not likely to get skunked, either. You can usually catch a few fish by pretending that the shoreline is the bank of a river and applying your stream expertise to these shallow areas of lakes.

The Bass Boat

Over the years, a specialized boat has come into favor for big lake fishing—the bass boat. But the bass boat is not limited to bass fishing alone; a lot of pan fish have been hoisted over the gunnels of bass boats,

FIGURE 12–3 A bass boat from Nordic. Note carpeted floor, pedestal seats, rod storage compartment, depth finder readout on console. (Courtesy Nordic Boat Company, Inc.)

as have catfish, walleyes, stripers, lake trout, and other game fish that thrive in still waters. What we have come to call a bass boat is basically a boat for finding fish in big water and doing it in a hurry while providing comfort to the anglers aboard.

The typical bass boat is sixteen to eighteen feet long, designed to accommodate two fishermen, or possibly three, if they're friendly. It has a beam of around fifty inches and a compromise hull design that provides some of the stability of the flat bottom, along with the planing efficiency necessary for high-speed cruising. Motors from thirty-five horses up are used, with motors of over a hundred horsepower finding favor on big lakes where a lot of distance must be covered in a hurry. Anglers who often fish in tournaments like these big outboards (or inboards in some cases), because they make it possible to race from one fishing spot to another; time wasted in transit is time that might better be devoted to catching a prize-winning fish.

Big motors provide a margin of safety, too. A sudden squall can make a big lake a very unpleasant place to be in a small boat. When you consider that some of the country's biggest lakes are found in parts of the country noted for violent thunderstorms and occasional tornadoes, the affection of anglers for the boat that can run at fifty to seventy miles an hour becomes understandable.

Bass boats have flat, carpeted floors, with storage compartments for gear, gasoline, and batteries. Upholstered pedestal seats are practically universal, and some of them are adjustable for height. Electric trolling motors are standard, too. Some anglers like the foot-controlled trollers, but those who do most of their casting standing up often prefer the hand-controlled models, which they learn to control with their knee while they stand. Most have rubber-coated anchors with remote-control systems for dropping and raising them. Sonar units are practically a necessity, and many boats run two or more transducers for reading at high speed or slow, or one for reading deep water, another for shallow sections.

Many of the accessories on the bass boat require electrical power. Big "deep-cycle" batteries power the trolling motor, while regular, cranking-style batteries provide the starting power for the big motors. Some motors have alternator units for recharging the starting battery while underway, but portable chargers at home are a necessity, especially for the trolling battery.

Bass boat fanciers disagree on the best material for constructing these boats. Aluminum boats are cheapest, and they're durable and relatively light. Fiberglass lends itself to making more interesting and efficient shapes, so most of the swoopy boats are made of this material. Fiberglass is less noisy than aluminum, too, but the use of carpeting in aluminum boats has negated some of that advantage.

Like other fishing tools, the bass boat is no better than its operator.

It's a complicated piece of machinery, and experience pays big dividends in its use. Some of the most elaborate bass boats can cost as much as a small house, and you're probably not ready for that just yet. Still, that's another good reason for going out with a guide now and then—you not only get to enjoy all the comforts of a bass boat, but you get to see how an expert takes advantage of the technology that has changed fishing so much in recent years.

Farm Pond Fishing

The jump from the bass boat to the farm pond is a move from the complicated to the simple, and, to most anglers, there are many days in the year when the simplicity of farm pond fishing is just what the doctor ordered. Many anglers learned how to fish in a farm pond, and that's still one of the best places for learning.

The typical farm pond is not very deep, so you have no need for sonar units, digital temperature probes, or chart recorders. Any kind of tackle you have handy will do, and if you need a boat at all, a small flat-bottom with a pole or a set of oars will suffice. And you'll probably have the pond to yourself most of the time.

Most farm ponds contain largemouth bass, and it's a rare farm pond that doesn't have at least one resident lunker that would be a trophy to make any fisherman proud. Farm ponds usually have lots of pan fish, often too many for the health of the population, so you can usually plan on a mess of tasty fillets after your return from a pond outing.

As in many other waters, spring and fall are the best times for farm pond fishing. In spring, the fish are on the spawning beds or in the pre- or post-spawning feeding sprees; in autumn, they're feeding heavily to put on weight for winter. During these periods, just about any lure, bait, or technique will work, so pick your favorite and go to it.

Midsummer is a different story. The pond is warm now, perhaps even hot, and the fish tend to sulk during the day. Now is the time for night fishing and for plug and bug fishing early and late. Bass bugging in farm ponds is practically a national pastime, and well it should be. When you see your bug disappear in a swirl and feel the bend a big largemouth can put in your favorite fly rod, you'll know why.

At times, farm pond fish will work right up to the edge of the pond seeking frogs and the aquatic insects that live in the vegetation that grows along the banks. You'll do well to stalk the bank carefully and keep a low profile, just as you would on a trout stream.

Farm ponds are common just about everywhere, and the majority of them are underfished. You'll probably find it easy to get permission from local farmers to fish their ponds, and if you provide them a mess of fish now and then (cleaned, of course), they'll be glad they let you fish their pond. When you get tired of the crowded trout streams and the whining bass boats on the big lakes, you should have little trouble finding good fishing and privacy at a nearby farm pond.

Farm ponds are only a small part of the total still water fishery resources available. With the combination of small ponds, natural lakes, and man-made impoundments, there's enough fishing for everyone who's interested with plenty of underfished, and even unfished, water left over. Your practice of still water fishing skills will pay big dividends.

CHAPTER 13

The Fishing
High and Dry

Sunday breakfast tastes terrific when you're thirteen years old. And this particular Sunday breakfast tasted even better than usual, because I knew it was to be followed by a fishing trip with my father. As Dad and I contentedly munched on our hotcakes and sausage, Mother spoke up with a bright idea.

"Bob, this would be a good day to tell David about the birds and the bees, don't you think?"

Dad made a sort of strangling sound with his hotcakes. "Uh . . . I don't know if . . ."

"Well, it seems like the perfect day. You'll be out there with nature, fishing and all. What could be a better setting? I think you should do it today."

Mom's voice had that edge of finality that indicated she expected the subject to be discussed. The rest of breakfast passed in near-silence, broken only by an occasional request for the syrup.

The car had been packed before breakfast, so when it was over Dad and I climbed in and drove off. Dad seldom played the radio, but this day he turned it on as soon as the engine started and kept fiddling with the knobs as we drove along. Neither of us knew what to say, so we said nothing.

We arrived at our destination an hour later, took the boat down off the car top carrier, and assembled our gear as we had so often before. I was grateful when the old Evinrude started; conversation was impossible as long as it was running. After a short run, though, Dad cut the engine, and we drifted silently into a cove at the edge of the little lake. He dropped his anchor, and I did the same with mine. Dad reached into the minnow bucket with a dip net, caught a minnow, and prepared to bait his hook. Suddenly he stopped, minnow in one hand, hook in the other.

"Is there anything you want to know about sex right now?"

"Not right now."

"But now that I've asked you, we've kind of talked about it, wouldn't you say?"

"I guess so."

"So if your Mom asks us if we've talked about it, we could say we have, right?"

"Right."

"Okay. Let's fish."

I didn't learn much about sex that day, much to my relief. Fact is, I already knew what Mom wanted explained to me, although my sources were probably not the ones she would have chosen. But I did learn something else that day, something that my Dad felt strongly about and that I have come to accept as a rule for my own fishing: Fishing is too important to be complicated by worldly problems. There is a time to think about serious things, and there is a time to fish, and the two should not be confused.

I remember another Sunday morning, fishing with my father, and this time we were accompanied by my uncle, Rod Sirbaugh. Rod loves to fish surface plugs, and he was a master at casting them into tight places, even with the bait-casting tackle of the 1950s. We drifted along while Rod cast to the shoreline, taking care to toss his plug tight to snags, downed trees, and other fishy-looking places. We drew within range of a downed tree lying in the water, and Rod dropped his plug right at the point where the wood disappeared under water. The plug vanished in a boil, Rod set the hook, and soon landed a smallmouth bass, a nice one of a pound and a half or so.

Dad dropped the anchor, and Rod made another cast to the tree. Bang! Another solid strike, and soon another bass on the stringer. Another cast, another fish. Another, and another. Our amazement grew with the length of the stringer of fish that Rod was accumulating. Still another cast, still another fish. In all, Rod made thirteen casts to that tree and landed thirteen bass, all well over the legal limit. It was the most amazing ten minutes of fishing I've ever seen, surely the best ten minutes of fishing in Rod's life. I was privileged to be there, and I've been privileged to recall the memory for thirty years.

These are two of my favorite angling memories, and I cite them to make the point first made by the fine angling writer, Sparse Grey Hackle, that much of the best fishing takes place far from water—in our minds and our memories, in lure making and fly tying, in passing along the skills of the angler to the coming generation, in the books that fishermen love, and in the conversation and sportsmen's clubs where we find companionship and an opportunity for service. So far, this book has been devoted to introducing you to the techniques and skills that you need to catch fish. This last chapter is based on the knowledge, universal among experienced anglers, that the catching is only a part of the total experience . . .

Tackle Tinkering

Many of the high and dry fishing hours you spend will be in making, repairing, maintaining, inspecting, and just (if the truth be told) playing with your equipment. Some of these activities can become hobbies themselves.

ROD BUILDING

Building your own fishing rod is not a difficult task, and it can provide a lot of satisfaction. There are a number of good books on the subject, and your local library might have at least one. If not, you can order a book through the tackle catalogs.

Make your first rod building kit an inexpensive one. If you're like most beginning rod builders, your second rod will be a lot better than your first, at least from an aesthetic standpoint, so save the expensive kit for when you have a little experience.

You can save up to half the cost of a high quality rod by assembling the components yourself. Once you have built a complete rod, you also have the skills to repair the other rods in your arsenal.

LURE MAKING

Many of the simpler lures can be made at home with the purchase of a few inexpensive tools. Jigs are the simplest, so they're a good choice to get started with. You'll need lead, molds for making the different shapes of jig heads (available in tackle shops and catalogs), a hot plate or stove for melting the lead, and a fly-tying vise for holding the jig while you attach the skirt. Toss in a few jig hooks, and you're set.

You can also make your own spinners. A number of mail order companies (Herter's, for one) sell the shafts, blades, beads, feathers, and hooks, along with instructions on how to assemble your own. With such a kit, you can assemble standard-type spinners or make up new creations of your own.

Making your own lures is not only fun, it can save a good deal of money. And you fish more aggressively when you know you can easily replace a lost lure.

FLY TYING

If you get interested in fly fishing, it's practically certain that you'll become a fly tier, too. Fly tying saves some money (at least that's a good excuse for getting started in it), but more importantly, fly tying gets you involved in the sport like nothing else does. Tying your own fly to represent some natural food you know the fish are feeding on, and then catching a fish with it, is one of the most satisfying experiences you'll ever have.

There are a host of good books on fly tying, and your local library probably has a couple of them. It's a good idea to do some reading before you start, because fly tying is complicated, and you'll need to find which aspects of it interest you the most. For example, if you want to tie flies for bass and pan fish, you'll need somewhat different materials than you would for trout flies.

There are a number of fly-tying kits on the market today, but most

FIGURE 13–1 The basic tools required for fly tying. (Photo by Katherine Lee)

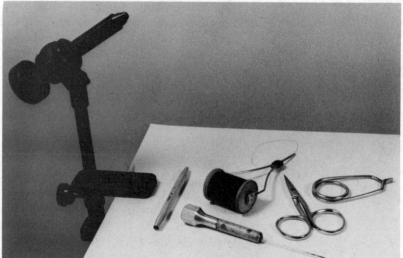

experienced tiers don't recommend them. A typical commercial kit contains a lot of junk materials that you'll probably never use. If you get a good kit, such as the one offered by Orvis, you'll spend more, but get your money's worth. An alternative to the kit approach is to buy your tools (fly-tying vise, scissors, hackle pliers, dubbing needle, and such) and then assemble the materials you need slowly as you learn to tie different types of flies.

Your best bet is to consult with an experienced tier. All the fly tiers I know are glad to help a beginner get started. Such a person can advise you on your tool and material needs, and might very well give you some excess fur and feathers to get you started. Above all, watch an experienced fly tier at work. The books are good, but experience at the side of a master is best, if you can manage it.

TACKLE MAINTENANCE

Even if you don't get into rod building or making your own lures, you'll want to protect your investment in your equipment by giving it good care. You'll find the mechanics of tackle maintenance can become a favorite off-season ritual.

Your rods should be stored in protective tubes and cloth rod bags. You can make the bags yourself if your rods didn't come with them.

FIGURE 13–2 The author's daughter, Meg, at age six, ties a fly. (Photo by Katherine Lee)

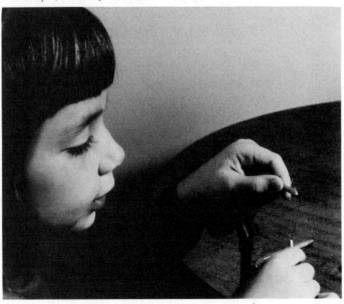

Aluminum rod tubes are available if you want to spend the twenty dollars or so they cost, but plastic tubes offer good protection at a much smaller price.

Reels should have bags, too, and you can make these as well. If you'd rather not go to the trouble, Seagram's Crown Royal whiskey comes in a cloth sack that fits most reels just fine. Remember to check the lines on your reels often and to change at the beginning of each season to new premium line. If you fish with fly tackle, store your fly lines off the reels over the off season. Winding them around fruit juice cans or quart mayonnaise jars will keep the line from retaining the tight kinks that come from being kept on the reel too long.

Rust is the main enemy of hooks and lures. Always dry your lures, hooks, and flies after fishing. A bag of the moisture-absorbing powder sold in hardware stores is good to keep in your tackle box.

These maintenance chores might sound like work, but you'll not find them so. When you can't be fishing in water, tackle-fussing makes it easy to fish in your mind.

On Teaching Children to Fish

Children younger than ten or so are not very well coordinated, especially in the small motor movements of fingers and hands that sophisticated tackle requires. For kids this age, spinning and spin casting is best for teaching the basics.

Size is an important consideration, since adult-sized tackle can be unwieldy for a youngster to handle. Consider one of the "mini" systems now available or a package system designed for small children, such as those in Figure 13–3.

TIME AND LOCATION

Fishing from shore is best for openers. Since it's safer than fishing from a boat, you will be able to concentrate on the fishing without the distraction of worrying about keeping the child in the boat. When the child's interest wanes, taking a walk or climbing a tree are easy alternative activities.

If possible in your area, take the child on a spring outing during the spawning period of local pan fish. To a child, fishing is *catching*, and spring sunnies are likely to be cooperative. With the little ones, the size of the fish and the difficulty of its capture are minor considerations; what counts with them is numbers, so the easier the fishing is the better. And children want to keep fish as evidence of their success. That's another good reason for concentrating on pan fish at the beginning.

FIGURE 13–3
A number of tackle companies make lightweight gear or tackle designed just for kids. (Photo by David Guiney)

BAIT OR LURE

Bait fishing is the traditional method for teaching kids to fish, and it's still a good one, since bait is likely to attract fish quickly. With children, you want to get that first fish on before their attention wanders. Bait shrimp is a good choice for a first outing, because it avoids the "Do I have to put that icky worm on the hook?" crisis.

If you choose to go the lure route, spinners are the best bet. They are easy to cast and don't foul often, and the casting and reeling gives the child something to do besides just waiting for action. Finally, the tendency of fish to hook themselves when they strike a spinner makes it likely that the child will hook and land any fish that hits. If the child is especially small, you can do the casting and hand the child the rod for the retrieve. My daughter Meg caught her first fish in exactly this way, at age three.

Whatever you do, don't plan to fish yourself when you take a child fishing for the first time. The idea is for the child to have the experience, and if you're not careful, you'll end up doing most of the fishing. It's

FIGURE 13–4
The first trophy (Photo courtesy U.S. Fish and Wildlife Service. Photo by Richard J. Blades)

better to swear off all but the demonstration casts right from the beginning.

Don't expect the child to have adult patience. The attention span of children is short, and they like action. It's entirely possible that you'll devote a couple of hours to organizing the trip and getting to the stream, only to find that the child wants to come home after ten minutes. That's why it's a good idea to go to an area where other activities are available. Sometimes you can do a little fishing, then do something else the child enjoys for a while, then fish some more.

Above all, don't pressure the child to like fishing just because you like it. It's true that fishing is the most popular pastime in the world, but it's also true that there are millions of people who have not the slightest interest in it. Perhaps the child you try to teach will turn out to be one of them. Remember that you fish to have *fun*. If other people have fun by not fishing, let them.

Whether teaching children or peers about fishing—and today's volunteer adult education programs offer the "expert" such opportunities—you may want to send for a two-part teaching aid kit available from the Sport Fishing Institute. Included are a teacher's guide and a poster-size chart depicting the conservation and the abuse of resources in two imaginary communities, Clear River Valley and Muddy River Valley. It explains the effects of human activities on soil, water, woods, and fish and game. It also describes a number of fish and animals, as well as the conditions under which they either live or die. The chart includes a strip of animals that can be cut out and pasted where they belong in the landscape.

The kit is available for about $1.75 (quantity discounts available) from the Sport Fishing Institute, 608 13th St. NW, Suite 801, Washington, DC 20005.

The Angling Literature

There are more than five thousand books on fishing printed in English, far more than have been written on any other sporting or recreation subject. Much of this work is of high literary quality. Reading angling classics and even collecting rare fishing books are hobbies that many fishermen enjoy.

It is a blessing that so many fine fishermen have been writers of elegant prose. Everyone knows and respects the work of Izaak Walton (although not many people actually *read* it!), but fishermen know that he has been followed by generations of fine writers including the Watermans, Schwieberts, and Haig-Browns of our own day.

One of the best ways to get into the angling literature of the past several centuries is to begin with Arnold Gingrich's *The Fishing In Print*

(Winchester Press, 1974). The book is a sampler and a guided tour through the best of angling writing, and Mr. Gingrich, the late editor of Esquire and a graceful angling writer himself, is eminently qualified to conduct it. The book provides a sample of writing by each of the greats, along with some historical and literary analysis, making it possible for the reader to fit each author into the historical context of fishing writing through the years. You won't like everything you find in the book, but you will no doubt meet some writers whose work you will wish to explore in more detail.

Conservation Organizations

Local and national clubs and conservation groups represent resources that you can benefit from and worthy efforts that you can contribute to. The Izaak Walton League, Trout Unlimited, BASS, The Federation of Fly Fishers, The American League of Anglers, and The Atlantic Salmon Federation are among the national organizations that you might be interested in joining and supporting. You'll probably find some local clubs in your area that are affiliated with some of these groups. You may also find some local sports clubs with no national attachments. These clubs provide you with the opportunity for association with men and women who share your love for the outdoors, and with the chance to serve the causes of conservation and environmental responsibility. Our fishing is constantly threatened, and organizations that work to preserve it deserve, indeed they require, the support of all anglers.

FIGURE 13–5 The pleasures of the off-season

In Conclusion

We've covered a lot of material in this book, although you'll find once you start fishing that we've just scratched the surface. But I hope our survey of freshwater fishing has convinced you to give it a try, and that you can now do so with the skills and knowledge you need to be successful. Most of all, I hope that fishing can bring to your life the challenge, relaxation, and contentment that it has brought to mine.

Tight lines!

APPENDIX **A**

Some Recommended Places to Fish

On the following pages, a number of the country's best anglers share some of their knowledge with you. I asked these fishermen to recommend a location or two where beginning anglers should have a good chance of success and to add their suggestions of tackle and techniques that should be successful.

Everything you need to know is here, including directions and the best times of year to go. Chances are that one or two of these spots are within easy travel of your home, so grab your gear and give one a try. Good luck!

JIM CORBIN

Caesar's Creek Lake (Ohio)

Jim Corbin makes his home in Yellow Springs, Ohio, where he is a research chemist by day and a custom rod maker by night. Jim fishes for bass and pan fish, relying on plug-casting, fly fishing, and spinning. Jim does his rod building in a solar-heated workshop that he designed and built himself. And he's an outdoor writer, too, having contributed an excellent series of articles on rod building to *Flyrodder Magazine*.

Recommended: Caesar's Creek Lake, Ohio

Directions: Access from Route 380, approximately ten miles south of Xenia. Route 73 also crosses the lower portion of the lake.

Best times of year: The fishing is good from April through early November. Morning and evening are best in the hot months. Sometimes large fish are taken at night. For current information on a day-to-day basis, contact Wildlife District Five, Xenia, OH 45385, or call (513) 372-7668.

Recommended techniques and equipment: Caesar's Creek Lake is fairly deep, so it is easier to fish from a boat. No boat rentals are available, so take your own or fish from the shore. A lake map (available for 30 cents from: Ohio Department of Natural Resources, Publications Dept., Fountain Square, Columbus, OH 43224) will show launch ramps.

Fly fishing: The lake has a lot of cover, particularly timber left standing when the lake was flooded. Work streamers and large bass bugs around shallow cover for both largemouth and smallmouth bass. For deeper water, go to a sinking or sink-tip line and work large streamers and nymphs. Small poppers, spiders, and nymphs work well on the pan fish population, especially from April to June.

Spinning/Plug Casting: Plastic worm and jig-and-eel combinations are effective over shallow cover. For deeper water, deep running plugs are the best bet.

179

DAN GAPEN

Cloquet River (Minnesota)

Dan Gapen is one of the country's most accomplished anglers. A leading tackle inventor (the "Bait Walker" sinker is his most recent), Dan is also an ardent conservationist; his work to protect running water led to his induction into the International Fishing Hall of Fame. Dan is a writer, too, with three books and numerous magazine articles to his credit. He lives in Big Lake, Minnesota, where he operates Gapen's World of Fishin', Inc., a company that produces a variety of freshwater and saltwater lures and terminal tackle items. Dan is a river fisherman, first and foremost.

Recommended: Cloquet River. The river is ninety-nine miles long. Dan considers the best section to be from Indian Lake south to the confluence with the St. Louis River.

Directions: The Cloquet is found twenty-five miles west of Duluth, on Highway 2 and Highway 53.

Best times of year: July, August, and September.

Recommended techniques and equipment: The Cloquet is a shallow river, best suited to float trips and casting. Anchored in the deeper sections, the live bait angler may catch channel catfish on minnows, leeches, or nightcrawlers. The casting angler will score on smallmouth bass, walleye, and northern pike.

Spinning: Light and semi-ultralight equipment is best. Five to five-and-a-half-foot rods, with light openface reels spooling six-pound line is the ticket. $1/16$- and $1/8$-ounce Ugly Bug lures in brown and yellow are effective, especially when tipped with a small piece of nightcrawler. Small dark fluorescent-colored crankbaits are good, too, in $1/4$- to $3/8$-ounce sizes.

Fly fishing: Seven- to eight-foot rods carrying seven- and eight-weight lines will match the conditions well. Popping bugs and streamers are the primary fly types needed.

Shallow-draft boats are ideal for the river, as are canoes. Motors are not necessary for floats unless upstream travel is anticipated.

DAN GAPEN

Upper Mississippi River

Recommended: The Upper Mississippi River. The Upper Mississippi constitutes 465 miles of running water from Itasca State Park to the northern suburbs of Minneapolis-St. Paul.

Directions: The river lies north and slightly west of Minneapolis. Much of the river runs parallel to State Highway 10. The best fishing is found in the lower 225 miles.

Best times of year: July, August, and September.

Recommended techniques and equipment: The Upper Mississippi is a smallmouth bass river, considered by Dan to be possibly the best in the country south of the Canadian border. Crayfish are the most predominant food source, and the angler can fish them live or represent them with lures. Five- to five-and-a-half-foot light action spinning rods with openface reels spooled with eight-pound line are recommended. Ugly Bug jigs in yellow, brown, or black are effective, as are dark-colored crankbaits in $1/4$-ounce size. Lures should be cast slightly upstream to represent the natural downstream movement of the natural food.

Bait fishing is successful with crayfish, nightcrawlers, and minnows. One of Dan's "Bait Walker" sinkers will help to hold the bait in place and out of trouble.

Shallow draft boats are a must for the Upper Mississippi. Fourteen-foot aluminum johnboats are best, with a six-horsepower motor.

181

REX GERLACH

Lake Havasu (Arizona)

Rex Gerlach spent nineteen years as a full-time freelance outdoor writer before settling down into his present job as Manager of Marketing Communications for Daiwa Corporation, one of the leading makers of rods and reels. Rex has fished and hunted all over the country, but his assignment in California with Daiwa led him to a fascination with fishing for freshwater striped bass in some of the big lakes of the West.

Recommended: Lake Havasu. The lake lies on the border of California and Arizona, so special fishing license regulations apply. Be sure to read fishing rules from both states before buying your license.

Directions: Lake Havasu is an impounded lake on the Colorado River. Arizona Route 95 runs close to the lake and offers access points.

Best times of year: All year, though fishing is slower during the winter.

Recommended techniques and equipment: As with other big lakes, hiring a guide is a good idea for your first outings. These fellows not only have the know-how, they have the equipment, including the fast boats and sonar chart recorders that are often necessary in locating and reaching striped bass.

Bait fishing: Shiners and shad are the ticket for the live bait angler, especially in winter when the fish are moody. A fast-taper, heavy action rod is desirable, one that can cast the minnow lightly and still have the backbone to fight fish that average three to five pounds and may run up to forty or more. Open-face spinning outfits are best, because the bail can be left open so that a fish picking up the bait will feel no resistance. Use line as light as conditions permit; six- or eight-pound test is good, unless you're fishing over heavy obstructions.

Plug-casting: Rex likes a five-and-a-half-foot medium-heavy rod for this fishing and a high-speed level-wind reel. Jigs and shad-finish crankbaits are effective with this equipment.

Spinning: Light-action spinning gear can be good in the winter when stripers chase small shad fry around. One-eighth- to 1/4-ounce jigs work well under these conditions.

Fly Fishing: Rex recommends a nine-foot rod for nine- or ten-weight line, and a reel that will hold the line along with 200 yards of backing. Surface feeding fish can be caught using a floating line and streamers or popping bugs. Deeper fishing will call for fast-sinking line or even lead-core fly line.

182

REX GERLACH

Lake Mead (Nevada)

Recommended: Lake Mead, Nevada. Lake Mead lies close to Las Vegas. The north shore is in Nevada, while the south shore is in Arizona. Check the special regulations before buying your license.

Directions: Take Route 95 south from Las Vegas to Route 93, then 93 to the lake. Or take 93 north from Kingman, Arizona. There are numerous boat launches and marinas on both shores of the lake.

Best times of year: Spring, summer, and fall. Winter fishing is slow.

Recommended techniques and equipment: Hire a guide the first time out. A boat is essential for striper fishing, a chart recorder highly desirable for locating the schools of fish.

Techniques and tackle discussed for Lake Havasu will apply here, too.

183

DICK KOTIS
Lake Erie (Ohio)

Dick Kotis is president of Fred Arbogast Company, Inc., of Akron, Ohio. Anglers everywhere know Arbogast as the makers of some of the most innovative and effective lures around, and Dick Kotis has been the creative force behind that effort for some time now. Dick enjoys all types of freshwater and saltwater fishing with light tackle, and he has done it in many parts of the world.

Recommended: The Western Basin of Lake Erie. Dick says this portion of the lake has the greatest concentration of walleyes on the North American continent.

Directions: The Western Basin can be reached anywhere from Port Clinton to Toledo, with access to these areas north from the Ohio Turnpike. Port Clinton has a number of sportfishing marinas that provide good access to the lake.

Best times of year: May 15 through August 1. June is the peak month.

Recommended techniques and equipment: Most anglers employ a charter boat and captain. The usual company is six anglers, so you might be able to round up some friends to make a day of it. Make sure the boat you charter is in good shape and radio-equipped; Lake Erie is very large and can be dangerous during bad weather.

The best beginner's technique for this walleye fishing is to use a spinner with a worm added. Use the countdown method to try different depths until you hit the level of the fish. The trick is to retrieve the spinner so that the blade just barely turns. Light action spinning or spin-casting gear is perfect, with 8- to 12-pound test line.

DICK KOTIS
Lake Michigan (Michigan)

Recommended: Lake Michigan and tributaries for salmon.

Directions: Manistee to Traverse City. Michigan Highway 22 parallels the lake for most of this distance, and both cities have large sport-fishing fleets.

Best times of year: August 1 through November 1.

Recommended techniques and equipment: Unless you have a lake-worthy boat yourself, this, too, will be a charter boat outing. Be sure that you hire a boat that has a depth finder, preferably one of the chart types that can locate schools or even large individual fish.

Use downriggers and trolling equipment, trolling bright spoons or lures. Lures that have a fast wobbling action are very effective.

ERIC PRICE

Little Deschutes River (Oregon)

Eric Price is president of Price's Anglers' Corner, a fly fishing specialty shop in La Pine, Oregon. Along with his father, Al Price, Eric developed the Price Vise, one of the premier fly-tying vises now on the market. As you might suspect, he's a fly fishing specialist.

Recommended: Little Deschutes River for brown trout.

Directions: The river flows all around La Pine, Oregon. Eric says you'll have a hard time getting in or out of town without crossing the river. La Pine itself is about thirty miles south of Bend, Oregon, on Route 97.

Best times of year: July and August.

Recommended techniques and equipment: Most any good fly fishing tackle will do. If you have a choice, an eight- or eight-and-a-half-foot rod for seven-weight line would be ideal.

The best fishing is with streamers and bucktails, so a sink-tip or sinking line might be a good idea to carry along with your standard floater. You'll fish from the bank for the most part; the river is deep and drops off too steeply for wading in most places.

ERIC PRICE

Fall River (Oregon)

Recommended: Fall River at Bend, Oregon, for dry fly fishing.

Directions: From La Pine, take Highway 97 north to Fall River cutoff, follow signs. From Bend, take Highway 97 south to cutoff.

Best times of year: July and August.

Recommended technique and equipment: This is dry fly fishing at its best, and light fly tackle is required. The Fall River is a spring creek with lots of fish, but it can require pretty delicate approaches and casting. A rod for six-weight line would be ideal.

Chest waders are recommended, as is mosquito repellent. Plan on using light tippets. Check with Price's Anglers' Corner or another nearby fly shop for the best patterns for flies at the time you go.

185

TOM ROSENBAUER

West Branch of the Ausable River (New York)

Tom Rosenbauer works for the Orvis Company in Manchester, Vermont. Orvis is one of the oldest and best purveyors of fine fly fishing and hunting equipment, and Tom's job is editor of *The Orvis News*, a regular newsletter to Orvis clients, which contains some of the best in outdoor writing, as well as informative material on fly fishing and bird hunting. Asked to describe his main fishing interest, Tom replies, "I'm interested in any species of fish that is foolish enough to bite a feathered hook!"

Recommended:	West Branch of the Ausable River, East of Lake Placid, New York.
Directions:	From Albany, take Interstate 87 north to Route 73. Take 73 north to Route 86, then 86 east to good fishing between Monument Falls and the town of Wilmington.
Best times of year:	Late May through October. Black flies are wicked until mid-July, but the terrific fishing compensates for them.
Recommended techniques and equipment:	This is ideal fly fishing for the beginner because the river is full of stocked rainbow and brown trout from seven to fifteen inches. Tom says the fishing is easy most of the time.

A six-weight fly rod from seven-and-a-half to nine feet is recommended, with a floating line. Large dry flies are effective: Tom recommends Royal Wulff, Ausable Wulff, and Haystack patterns in sizes 10 and 12. Montana and Hare's Ear nymphs are effective, too, in sizes 8-12, as is a small Muddler Minnow in the same sizes. Late in the season, you can have good midge fishing in the slow pools with black and cream midge patterns in sizes 20-24.

Tom recommends that beginners avoid the difficult wading in fast, boulder-strewn water; there are plenty of shallow pools in between the rough portions. And felt-soled waders and a wading staff are musts—the bottom is treacherously slippery.

TOM ROSENBAUER

Yellow Breeches Creek (Pennsylvania)

Recommended: The Yellow Breeches Creek, in particular the Allenberry water near Boiling Springs, Pa.

Directions: From Interstate 81 at Carlisle, take Route 34 to Boiling Springs. Ask directions to Allenberry Resort, site of flies-only, fish-for-fun area.

Best times of year: May through October.

Recommended techniques and equipment: The Allenberry stretch of the Yellow Breeches is some of the most hallowed trout water in America. Its fishing is usually challenging, often frustrating, but always enjoyable. The fish are rainbow trout with a few browns available, too, and they are sophisticated fish that have seen all the angler's tricks. Beginners can still catch them by careful wading and delicate casting.

A six-weight fly rod is about right here, and many regulars use four- and five-weight outfits. A nine-foot leader tapered to 5X is typical. Chest waders are recommended, but you can get away with hip boots if those are all you have. Felt soles are a good security measure, although the water is not difficult for wading.

Before fishing, stop at the Yellow Breeches Fly Shop in Boiling Springs for recommended fly patterns and techniques. Standard dry flies like the Adams are good, and ant patterns work well all summer. Hare's Ear nymphs are effective below the Allenberry Dam, and streamers are good, too, especially a black Wooly Bugger. Check to see if specific insects are hatching, so you can get what you need to "match the hatch."

In October, spawning trout move into the outflow from Boiling Springs Lake, and you can fish over big rainbows and brook trout. Allenberry offers delightful accommodations, good food, and a playhouse as well.

RAY SCOTT

Santee-Cooper Lakes (South Carolina)

Ray Scott is founder and president of the Bass Anglers Sportsman Society, the world's largest fishing organization with more than 400,000 members. BASS pioneered professional bass fishing and now sponsors eight national tournaments with a total prize value of $650,000. Scott introduced the "catch-and-release" concept to tournament bass fishing by requiring that competing anglers keep their catch alive and release them after completion of the tournament. Ray provided the following information from the pages of *Bassmaster Magazine*, one of the publications produced by his organization.

Recommended: The Santee-Cooper Lakes (Lakes Marion and Moultrie) in South Carolina.

Directions: From Columbia, SC, Interstate 95 crosses the lower portion of Lake Marion.

Best times of year: Late March through early June.

Recommended techniques and equipment: Spinning and casting tackle are most popular here, with 15-pound test line used on the average spinning outfit and 20-pound on the casting gear. Bass here can top ten pounds, so heavy equipment is justified. Fly rods and popping bugs are popular for morning and evening fishing, especially in spring and fall.

Spoons, spinnerbaits, and six- to eight-inch plastic worms work best in the early season, with brown and dark blue the favored worm colors. Summer angling calls for silver-colored spinnerbaits and buzz baits in addition to these.

The Santee-Cooper Lakes offer striped bass, catfish, and big crappies, as well as largemouth bass.

RAY SCOTT

Toledo Bend Reservoir (Louisiana)

Recommended: Toledo Bend Reservoir on the Louisiana-Texas border.

Directions: On the east side of the reservoir, numerous access roads are available off Highway 171. On the west side, look for access off Highway 96.

Best times of year: March through April and mid-August through mid-November.

Recommended techniques and equipment: Medium action bait-casting gear is favored for early season largemouth fishing with ten- to seventeen-pound line. Lighter equipment comes into vogue for difficult summer fishing. Crayfish colored crank baits are good for early season fishing, as are green and black plastic worms. Purple worms work better in summer. In fall, spinnerbaits in white pay off, as do jig-and-eel or jig-and-worm combinations.

Peak spawning takes place during the first two weeks in April. At that time the fish will usually be in water of seven feet or less, close to brush, stickups, or logs. In summer, the fish are deeper, often found over underwater humps and ridges 12–14 feet down.

Toledo Bend provides good striper and crappie fishing, too.

RAY SCOTT

Truman Reservoir (Missouri)

Recommended: Truman Reservoir, west-central Missouri.

Directions: Take most direct route to Clinton, Osceola, or Warsaw; these three towns offer best access to the lake. Clinton and Osceola are on Highway 13, Warsaw on Route 65.

Best times of year: April and May, October and November.

Recommended techniques and equipment: Truman Reservoir has lots of standing timber, and you'll need stout equipment to horse hooked bass out of the woods. Medium to heavy action rods are most popular, with fourteen- to seventeen-pound line. Really heavy lines are not used much because of the clarity of the water.

Spinnerbaits, topwater plugs, jigs, worms, and crankbaits all score well in the early season. Plastic worms come into their own in summer and early fall. Fly rodders can do well in morning and evening.

Truman is still a comparatively new reservoir with a developing fishery that is not yet completely understood. In addition to largemouth bass, the impoundment features striped bass, crappie, white bass, bluegill, catfish, and tiger muskies (musky-northern pike hybrid).

APPENDIX **B**

Periodicals for the Angler

Anglers have available to them not only books but a large and rapidly growing group of magazines, many of them aimed exclusively at fishermen. No matter what your preferred method of fishing, one or more of the following magazines will enhance your fishing pleasure and success.

Angler Magazine: Bi-monthly. Published by Angler Publications, 285 Horner Avenue, Suite 5, Oakland, CA 94604. Good writing and broad coverage of the angler's interests.

Bassmaster Magazine: Bi-monthly. Published by B.A.S.S., Box 17900. Montgomery, AL 36117. This is the official magazine of Ray Scott's Bass Anglers Sportsman's Society, available to members only. There are no newsstand sales. Bass fishing, particularly largemouth, particularly in Southern impoundments.

Field and Stream: Monthly. CBS Publications, Consumer Publishing Group, 1515 Broadway, New York, NY 10036. Founded in 1895, this is the granddaddy of the outdoor magazines, and still one of the best.

Excellent writing and frequent how-to and where-to articles on hunting as well as fishing. A regional section spotlights areas of the country, and Gene Hill's column is usually worth the price of the magazine all by itself.

Fishing Facts: Monthly. Published by Northwoods Publishing, Box 609, Menomonee Falls, WI 53051. Emphasis here is on the rivers and lakes of the upper Midwest. Dan Gapen is a frequent contributor, as is Buck Perry, the popularizer of "structure" fishing.

Fishing World: Bi-monthly. Published by Allsports Publishing Co., 51 Atlantic Avenue, Floral Park, NY 11001. Good coverage of both fresh-water and saltwater angling.

Fly Fisherman Magazine: Published six times a year by Historical Times, Inc. 2245 Kohn Road, P.O. Box 8200, Harrisburg, PA 17105. The first of the magazines aimed strictly at fly anglers, *Fly Fisherman* is still regarded by most fly fishers as the best. The most distinguished fly fishermen write regularly for the magazine, and the coverage of the sport is international in scope.

Flyfishing: Bi-monthly. Published by Frank Amato Publications, P.O. Box 02112, Portland, OR 97202. Formerly *Flyfishing the West*, this magazine has recently assumed a national scope. The slant is still some-what toward the Western fly angler, but the technical information will benefit fly anglers anywhere. Fearless product evaluations are among the features of the magazine.

Flyrodder: Published six times a year by Flyrodder Publishing Co. Inc., 10457 Storybook Drive, Cincinnati, OH 45242. Aimed at the Midwestern and Eastern fly angler, this magazine emphasizes the warm-water applications of the sport, with regular articles on fishing with fly tackle for bass and panfish. Trout are not neglected, though, and how-to articles on rod-building and fly tying are regularly included.

Fly Tyer: Quarterly. Published by Fly Tyer, Inc., Box 1231, Route 16, North Conway, NH 03860. Fly tying and nothing but fly tying. Con-tributors and regular columnists represent the best fly tiers in the world. A must magazine for the fanatical fly tier.

Gray's Sporting Journal: Quarterly. Published by Gray's Sporting Journal, Inc., 42 Bay Road, South Hamilton, MA 01982. The class act of the outdoor periodicals. Most of the articles on hunting and fishing are not technical or "how-to"; the emphasis is on why we love the outdoors and the sports that are appropriate to it. Superb writing and graphics and the best of outdoor art are featured. Back issues rapidly become collec-tor's items.

Hooks and Lines: Bi-monthly. Published by the International Wom-en's Fishing Association, Box 2825, Palm Beach, FL 33480. Women anglers have their own magazine by joining this organization. No newsstand sales.

In-Fisherman: Bi-monthly. Published by Al Lindner's Outdoors, Inc., P.O. Box 999, Rt. 8, Brainerd, MI 56401. Freshwater techniques emphasized here, especially those appropriate to the natural lakes and streams of the upper Midwest. Superb illustrations, outstanding technique articles, up-to-date coverage of the latest in fishing trends and equipment. A must for the walleye and smallmouth bass angler. One of the best.

Outdoor Life: Monthly. Published by Times-Mirror Magazines, Inc., 380 Madison Avenue, New York, NY 10017. One of the Big Three outdoor periodicals. Hunting and fishing articles with a regional insert that offers tips and guides to hot spots in your area. The loss of Lefty Kreh as a regular columnist has hurt, but Fishing Editor Jerry Gibbs is knowledgable and writes well.

Salmon, Trout, Steelheader: Bi-monthly. Published by Frank Amato Publications, P.O. Box 02112, Portland, OR 97202. The title tells it all; aimed at the Western angler using all methods for trout, salmon, and steelhead.

The American Fly Fisher: Quarterly. Published by the Museum of American Fly Fishing, Manchester, VT 05254. Articles of historical interest to fly fishermen. Collectibles, museum pieces, old angling literature and art are featured. Guarding the tradition of fly angling. No newsstand sales.

The Atlantic Salmon Journal: Quarterly. Official publication of The Atlantic Salmon Federation, 1434 St. Catherine St. W. Suite 109, Montreal, Quebec, Canada H3G1R4. Salmon fishing stories and information, with contributors and articles on fishing in Newfoundland, Nova Scotia, New Brunswick, Great Britain, and Ireland. No newsstand sales.

The Flyfisher: Quarterly. Published by The Federation of Flyfishers, International Headquarters, P.O. Box 1088, West Yellowstone, MT 59888. The emphasis here is on the experience of fly fishing, although there are some technical articles. High-quality art and color photos are featured, and Steve Raymond's book reviews are the best anywhere in evaluating recent titles in fly fishing. Available only to associate members of FFF. No newsstand sales.

Trout: Quarterly. The official publication of Trout Unlimited, P.O. Box 1944, Washington, DC 20013. All methods are covered here, but the emphasis is on trout only. Subscriptions automatic with membership in TU. No newsstand sales.

Sports Afield: Monthly. Published by Hearst Magazines, 280 W. 55th St., New York, NY 10019. The brightest and most stylish of the Big

193 Three. Superb color reproduced on high quality paper distinguishes *Sports Afield.* Good writing, too, and lots of tips in special insert section. Regular columnist Mark Sosin is one of the country's most knowledgable anglers, especially in light tackle and fly angling in salt water.

Southern Outdoors: Bi-monthly. B.A.S.S. Publications, Inc. No. 1 Bell Road, Montgomery, AL 36141. Freshwater and saltwater angling, along with hunting, in the southern U.S. is the angle here. The fishing stories run heavily to warm-water species, but there are occasional articles on the growing trout fishery in the South, most of it provided by cold-water releases from the big impoundments. A high-quality magazine, and still improving.

In addition to these magazines, don't overlook regional and state publications. There are many good ones; *The Pennsylvania Angler* and *The Florida Sportsman* are two of the best, but don't overlook others. And many states feature yearly fishing publications, some of them sponsored by state fish and game agencies, which will give the novice angler the rundown on local conditions and techniques.

Glossary

anadromous   A technical term for those fish that move back and forth between fresh and salt water. Most typical are those that are hatched in fresh water, eventually go to the sea to mature, then return to fresh water to reproduce.

arbor knot   A knot for fastening fishing line to reel spools.

back cast   That portion of a fly cast in which the line is cast above and behind the angler.

backing   Line used to build up the spool core under the primary fishing line. Backing aids in casting by filling the spool and protects against the long run of a big fish.

backlash   A line snarl common with bait-casting tackle.

bail   A metal device that is activated by the handle on a spinning reel. When it turns, it winds line on the spool.

bank   A type of molded sinker in which a hole for attaching the line is molded into the top of the sinker.

194

barb   A raised sliver of metal behind the point of a fish hook. The barb is intended to keep the hook from backing out once the point has penetrated.

barbules   Fleshy appendages around the mouths of certain fish, which combine the senses of taste, feeling, and, sometimes, smell.

barrel swivel   A type of swivel with eyes on either end for attaching fishing line and barrel-shaped swivel in the middle for reducing line twist. Unlike snap swivels, which are attached at the end of the fishing line, barrel swivels are attached somewhere within the line, as in attaching a shock leader to a lighter-weight line.

bend   The curved portion of the hook, which begins at the shank and ends at the point. Some hook bends are perfectly round and some are parabolic.

blood knot   A knot used to tie together two strands of fishing line. When used with monofilament, the blood knot is reliable only when used with strands of similar diameter.

bobber   A float to hold a bait at a selected depth and to signal the strike of a fish.

brackish water   Slightly salty water, most often found in estuaries where fresh water and salt water meet.

brush anchors   An anchor that is attached to tree limbs or brush. Brush anchors provide an overhead anchoring point, an important safety feature where sudden changes in water level are common.

bucktails   Flies designed to represent bait fish. Bucktails are tied with the hair from the tail of a deer.

bug taper   A special taper in fly lines in which the weight of the line is concentrated near the front, enhancing casting distance when using large, air-resistant flies.

butt   The heaviest portion of a leader. In fly fishing, the butt section is the portion attached to the fly line. Also, the part of a fishing rod closest to the hand grip.

caddisflies   A group of aquatic insects with a complete life cycle. Deposited in the stream as eggs, they grow into larvae, most of which build for themselves characteristic cases that adhere to rocks and other features of the stream bottom. Eventually the larvae pupate, following which they migrate to the surface and emerge as winged adults. Fly anglers represent all of these stages, and live bait fishermen sometimes use the larvae as bait.

catch-and-release   A form of angling in which fish are landed and then released to be available to be caught again another day. Regulations require catch-and-release on certain trout streams and in many bass tournaments.

cover   A general term applying to those physical features that provide protection to fish. Rocks, weed beds, undercut banks, and depth all provide cover.

crankbait   A plug with an action brought out by reeling. Crankbaits are usually sinking or diving plugs that wiggle from side to side when retrieved.

crayfish   A lobster-like crustacean that lives in many freshwater streams and is a favorite food of game fish.

crawdad   Common name for the crayfish.

dapping   The practice of dropping a light bait or fly softly onto the surface of the stream, in imitation of the alighting of a grasshopper, cricket, or other insect.

dipsey   A teardrop-shaped sinker with a wire loop to which the line is attached.

disturbers   A group of plugs that attract fish by disturbing the water's surface as they are manipulated.

double-taper   A fly line taper in which each end of the line gradually tapers down to a fine point. Double-taper lines allow for delicate presentation of the fly and are economical, since they can be reversed.

dough balls   Bait for carp and catfish. Doughballs may be bought commercially or made at home from many different recipes.

downrigger   A device for presenting baits or lures to fish at depths of one hundred feet or more. The downrigger consists of a reel that allows a weight to be lowered on a wire. The actual fishing line is attached just above the weight with a special clip that frees the line from the downrigger when a fish is hooked.

drag   1. A mechanical device that provides adjustable resistance to the turning of a reel spool. The reel drag makes it possible for the reel to yield line rather than breaking it. 2. In fly fishing, the unnatural movement of an artificial fly when it is pulled across the current. Drag ordinarily causes fish to shun the fly, because it is behaving in an unnatural manner.

dropper   An extra strand on a leader allowing the angler to fish an additional fly or to attach split shot that can be easily removed. Also, the name given to an extra fly attached to the leader in this way.

dry flies   Flies designed to float on the surface of the water. Most dry flies are intended to represent the adult forms of aquatic insects.

emergence   The point in the development of aquatic insects at which they become winged, air-breathing creatures.

eye   The portion of a fishhook that is tied to the line. On most hooks, the eye is formed by bending the hook wire around in a circle.

false casting   In fly casting, continuing the alternation between back cast and forward cast without allowing the fly to fall. False casting is used to measure out line needed to reach a particular target or to flick the moisture off a dry fly.

feathering the line   A technique for slowing or stopping the flight of a lure cast from a spinning or casting rod. A finger or thumb pressing on the reel spool alters the rate of line flow and thus affects the flight and distance of the lure or bait.

floating-diving plug   A hollow plug with an angled lip that floats at rest and dives when retrieved.

free-spool   In bait-casting equipment, a mode in which the reel spool is released from the internal gearing and allowed to spin freely. The free-spool release button is usually engaged during casting and may also be used during bait fishing, so that a fish that moves with the bait will not feel reel resistance.

gap (also "gape")   In a fishhook, the distance between the point and the shank. The gap is the customary basis for sizing hooks.

grilse   Immature Atlantic salmon, returning to fresh water for the first time.

Handy Andy   A type of fishing tackle pack that incorporates two bags connected by shoulder straps. One bag hangs on the angler's chest; the other, down the back.

hellgrammite   Common name for the larvae of the dobsonfly. The hellgrammite is a wonderful live bait, particularly for bass.

hook disgorger   A tool for removing hooks too deeply ingested by fish to be reached by the fingers alone.

hypothermia   A sudden and rapid loss of body heat brought on by evaporation, which follows a wetting of the body. Hypothermia can lead to coma and death.

impoundment   An artificial lake created by the damming of a stream.

improved clinch knot   A basic knot for attaching lures, flies, swivels, hooks, and snaps to fishing line.

jig   A simple lure in which a lead head is combined with a skirt or tail of soft feathers, rubber, or plastic.

kirbed   In fishhooks, an offset of the point from the shank. Kirbed hooks are offset from the right, as viewed from the hook eye.

lateral line   The bundle of nerves along a fish's side that respond to vibrations transmitted through the water. In many species, the lateral line is visible as a dark stripe.

leader   Any section of fishing line between the primary line and the bait or lure. Leaders are usually of monofilament and are most common in fly fishing.

mayflies   A group of insects that spend most of their lives living underwater and breathing through gills, then emerge as winged insects, mate, lay eggs to begin the cycle again, and then die. Mayflies are represented by the fly fisherman at all of these life stages.

minnow harness   A device for lashing a live minnow to a hook. A harness may keep a minnow lively longer than being impaled on the hook. More often, the harness is used to make it possible to cast a minnow repeatedly, as if it were a lure.

monofilament   Fishing line made of nylon drawn in a single strand.

multiplying reel   A reel in which gears multiply the action of the reel handle, so that each turn of the handle produces more than one turn of the spool. All casting reels have multiplication. A few fly reels are multipliers, too.

nymph   The angler's term for the immature underwater forms of certain aquatic insects, including mayflies, stoneflies, damselflies, and dragonflies. Some nymphs can be used as live bait, but more often they are represented artificially by the fly angler.

overhead cast   A cast in which the lure or bait is cast directly or nearly directly overhead in a vertical plane.

plug   A type of lure that either represents the shape of game fish prey or creates a disturbance on the surface or under the surface to attract the fish. The first plugs were carved of wood, but most modern plugs are of hard or soft plastic.

plug-casting   Another name given to revolving-spool bait-casting tackle.

popping plug   A topwater plug with a concave face that pops or gurgles when manipulated.

pounds test   A measure of the breaking strength of fishing line. The pounds test of a given line is the amount of strain, measured in pounds, required to break the line.

prime lie   A location that offers fish the opportunity for feeding, while also providing protection and relief from stress.

put-and-take   The process of stocking hatchery fish in a stream in the expectation that they will be caught quickly rather than establishing a resident population in the stocked area.

pyramid   A sinker shaped like a pyramid, with a wire loop on the flat side for attaching the line.

retrieve   Any method by which the angler brings a fly or lure back to be recast. The retrieve is usually designed to lure fish into striking and may involve pauses, twitches, changes of speed, and other techniques.

reversed   In fish hooks, an offset of the point from the shank. A reversed hook is offset from the left, as viewed from the hook eye.

rock worms   A common name for the larvae of caddisflies. They are worm-like in appearance and live in cases on the bottom of stream rocks.

roll cast   A fly cast used when obstructions prevent a normal back cast. The angler draws the line toward him on the water and then rolls it out again.

seine   A specialized net for collecting hellgrammites and other bottom-dwelling baits. Basically a section of screen with supporting structure, the seine is held in the current while the bottom upstream is disturbed, sending bait into the seine.

shock leader   A leader designed to absorb shock or abrasion in fighting big fish. A shock leader varies from a few inches to a few feet in length and is always of heavier material than the primary fishing line.

shank   The portion of a fishhook between the eye and the bend.

side cast   A cast made in a horizontal plane. The side cast is used when obstructions prevent an overhead cast or when the lure or bait must be cast back under overhanging branches or other obstacles.

sinker   A lead weight that is used to take or hold a bait close to or on the bottom.

siltation   The process by which soil erodes from the land and is washed into lakes and streams. Siltation degrades game fish habitat.

single-action reel   A reel that has no gearing: one turn of the handle produces one turn of the spool. Most fly reels are single-action.

sinking plugs   A group of plugs that are heavier than water and designed to be fished under the surface.

snake guides   Simple wire guides in which a single strand of wire is twisted to form an opening for line. Snake guides are common on fly rods.

snap swivel   A combination of a safety-pin type snap and a swivel, which allows the fastening of lures to fishing line. The swivel reduces the tendency of spinning lures to foul the line.

snelled hook   A hook already attached to a short length of monofilament.

spawning   The act of reproduction in fish, where the female releases eggs that are fertilized by the milt (sperm) of the male.

spoon   A flat lure, shaped somewhat like a tablespoon, which attracts fish through a wobbling action. Most spoons are of highly polished chrome or brass, but some are enameled.

spin casting   A form of casting in which a stationary reel spool, mounted on top of the rod, is enclosed in a housing from which the line passes out through a small hole. A push button releases line during the cast, and a metal or ceramic pin respools the line when the reel handle is operated.

spinner   A lure that attracts fish by the revolution of flashing metal blades.

spinnerbait   A lure that combines a jig and a spinner. The jig rides on the bottom, a flashing spinner blade rides on top, and the line is attached to a wire in between the two.

spinning   A method of casting in which the line is cast from a stationary reel spool, mounted so that the line peels off the end of the spool during the cast.

split shot   Small round lead balls with a split in one side. The line is inserted in the split and the shot squeezed tightly around it.

stoneflies   A group of insects that spend most of their lives living under water and breathing through gills. At maturity, they emerge by crawling out onto streamside rocks and other debris, splitting their nymphal shucks and becoming winged adults. Later, they mate, and the females deposit eggs into the stream. Fly anglers imitate all of these stages, and the nymphs are sometimes used as live bait.

streamers   Flies tied to represent bait fish. Streamers are tied with feathers on long-shanked hooks.

stripper guide   The guide on a rod closest to the reel and handle.

surgeon's knot   A knot used to tie together two strands of fishing line. The surgeon's knot is especially good for two strands of widely differing diameter.

surgeon's loop   A modification of the surgeon's knot that produces a loop.

taper   The diameter configuration of a fly line. Tapered lines vary in diameter according to their purpose in casting.

thermal stratification   The process by which water in lakes separates into layers of different temperatures.

three-way swivel   A swivel with three eyes for attaching fishing line. With such a swivel, the main line can be attached to one eye, the baited hook to a second, and a sinker to the third. Or two baits or lures can be attached and fished from one line.

throat In a fishhook, the distance between the point and the deepest portion of the bend. The throat represents the maximum depth of the hook's penetration.

tippet The end of the leader to which the fly or lure is tied.

tiptop The last guide, at the very tip of the rod.

treble hook A hook that has three bends, three points, and three barbs, all sharing a common shank and eye.

trolling A method of fishing in which lures or bait are pulled behind a moving boat propelled by a motor, oars, or wind.

tube knot A knot for attaching a leader butt to a fly line.

Index

203